BILL VIOLA

This book was published on the occasion of the exhibition "Bill Viola," organized by the Whitney Museum of American Art.

Exhibition Itinerary

Los Angeles County Museum of Art	November 2, 1997–January 11, 1998
Whitney Museum of American Art, New York	February 12–May 10, 1998
Stedelijk Museum, Amsterdam	September–November, 1998
Museum für Moderne Kunst, Schirn Kunsthalle, and Karmeliterkloster, Frankfurt	January–April, 1999
San Francisco Museum of Modern Art	June 4–September 7, 1999
The Art Institute of Chicago	October 16, 1999–January 16, 2000

This exhibition is sponsored by V E B A

Significant support has also been provided by Peter and Eileen Norton and the Peter Norton Family Foundation, with additional funding from Pamela and Richard Kramlich, Marion Stroud Swingle, Lynn Forester, Barbara Wise, and the National Committee of the Whitney Museum of American Art.

Research for the exhibition and publication was supported by income from an endowment established by Henry and Elaine Kaufman, The Lauder Foundation, Mrs. William A. Marsteller, The Andrew W. Mellon Foundation, Mrs. Donald A. Petrie, Primerica Foundation, Samuel and May Rudin Foundation, Inc., The Simon Foundation, and Nancy Brown Wellin.

700.92
V795

Curated by David A. Ross and Peter Sellars

BILL VIOLA

With contributions by Lewis Hyde, Kira Perov, David A. Ross, and Bill Viola

Whitney Museum of American Art · New York
in association with
Flammarion · Paris · New York

LIBRARY
UNIVERSITY OF ST. FRANCIS
JOLIET, ILLINOIS

Sponsor's Statement

VEBA, the world's largest utility-based conglomerate and Germany's fourth largest company, takes pride in sponsoring the first major international survey of Bill Viola's art, organized by the Whitney Museum of American Art.

Through his single-channel videos and multimedia installations, Viola has established himself among the truly independent and accomplished artists in contemporary America. He integrates state-of-the-art technology with audiovisual elements to craft deeply spiritual and contemplative works, capturing the essence of death, birth, and a variety of transcendent experiences of life.

The exhibition will travel across the US, from Los Angeles to New York, and then open in Amsterdam and Frankfurt before returning to San Francisco and then Chicago. As the principal sponsor, VEBA is honored to bring this innovative artist's most important works to six major metropolitan areas in America and Europe. We at VEBA hope that "Bill Viola" will enrich the cultural lives of people on two continents, as it extends a cultural bridge over the Atlantic.

VEBA's sponsorship of the exhibition affirms our belief in the value of intercultural exchange and, at the same time, signals our increased focus on internationalization and our ongoing commitment to the US.

Ulrich Hartmann
Chairman of the Board of Management and CEO
VEBA

Contents

A Feeling for the Things Themselves

David A. Ross

"It is not the language of painters but the language of nature, which one should listen to....The feeling for things themselves, for reality, is more important than the feeling for pictures."

—Vincent Van Gogh, 1882 [1]

"...modern European art endeavors to represent things as they are themselves, Asiatic and Christian art to represent things more nearly as they are in God, or nearer their source."

—A.K. Coomaraswamy, 1934 [2]

Twenty-six years ago I was appointed curator of video art at the Everson Museum in Syracuse, New York. At the time, I only suspected that my title was unique, but it soon became apparent that I was the first museum curator devoted to this new art form. During the years I held that position and throughout my early professional career, I witnessed first-hand the birth and development of a field now known simply as video art. As a curator with often conflicting responsibilities—to promote an awareness of this new art form and to elaborate its critical and theoretical framework—I have watched the medium move from the periphery of the art world to its center, particularly within art museums. Of equal importance has been the extent to which artists working with video have redefined our idea of television as a creative medium. A whole new generation of artists now uses video like a pencil, as John Baldessari predicted would happen.

Baldessari made his prediction in the early 1970s, in a pre-cable TV, pre-Internet culture, when video was considered a revolutionary art medium. At the time, I felt something especially satisfying about work-

ing with artists whose creative output held implications that extended beyond the cloistered world of art history. This was an extraordinary moment, when the idea of making history seemed unavoidable, and meaningful cultural revolution seemed possible. It was a moment when that special demographic bulge known as the American postwar baby boom generation finally began to sense its power to change the existing order of things; when artists angrily and rather summarily rejected what seemed to be the deadening conditions of an art world bounded by money and privilege; when previously marginalized artists found ways to assert themselves within once-closed worlds.

Art historically, the 1970s were defined by Conceptualism and Post-minimalism, two intersecting attitudes toward the making of art in which ontological and phenomenological concerns were played out in traditional media like painting and drawing, and often in nontraditional sculptural media, including video, photography, and performance. Since these attitudes were progressive and essentially non-exclusionary, a wide-ranging group of artists, musicians, filmmakers, choreographers,

1. Vincent Van Gogh, *The Complete Letters of Vincent Van Gogh* (Greenwich, Connecticut: The New York Graphic Society, 1958).

2. A.K. Coomaraswamy, *The Transformation of Nature in Art* (1934; ed. New York: Dover Publications, 1956), pp. 30–31.

Nam June Paik
From *Global Groove*, 1973
Videotape, color; 30 minutes

and poets took pleasure in making art that defied traditional definition and erased the boundaries among media. It was a period when there was a longing to explore new ways of representing the real.

This was the moment when James Harithas, then the director of the Everson Museum, hired me to be his video curator, and I subsequently hired Bill Viola, an artist and electronic musician, to work with me.[3] His technical skills and artist's intuition were invaluable, and in many ways he functioned more as my partner than my assistant. For both of us it was an amazing period of exploration. Since that time, Viola has emerged as a key figure in a generation of artists who employ advanced electronic image and sound technologies to produce works of art. Today, his video installations are highly sought-after by museums and private collectors, his single-channel video works have been commissioned and broadcast around the world, and his writings have been published and anthologized internationally.

Viola and I left Syracuse in the early 1970s and went our separate ways.

As I moved from one museum curatorial position to another, my attitudes toward video art changed markedly. To a certain extent, I lost interest in the community of artists defined by video qua video, and in the pure technical wizardry produced by many video enthusiasts. More important, I began to evaluate video within a broader set of aesthetic contexts, no longer privileging its technological novelty or implicit ideological stance. I turned instead to a small group of artists who were making works not as "video artists," but as artists who happened to use video. Bill Viola was at the core of this group. Moreover, like others of this generation of artists and critics, I found myself engaged in art that explored notions of the observable world and proposed new ways of understanding our complex perception of what is real.

So for me, the consideration of Viola's work is somewhat more complex than the simple reflection on his history as part of the first generation of video artists. When he was still working at the Everson Museum, Viola was already closely involved with the avant-garde composer and musician David Tudor.[4] As a young artist well-versed in the use and

---

3. Viola worked as a video preparator at the Everson Museum of Art in the early 1970s, and assisted Peter Campus and this author on the presentation of the Campus survey exhibition at the Everson in 1974. In addition, from 1974 to 1976, Viola worked in Florence, Italy, at an independent art video production facility, Art/Tapes/22, run by Maria Gloria Conti Bicocchi. During this period, he also worked with a remarkable group of European and American artists, including Giulio Paolini, Joan Jonas, Vito Acconci, Jannis Kounellis, and others.

4. Early in his career, Viola was part of David Tudor's Rainforest ensemble. The experience of working with Tudor and the other musicians in the group was extremely influential on his subsequent development, as Tudor's chaos-based music, and especially the notion of making music with (and through) found objects directed Viola further into work with things and images taken from the real world, transformed, and returned back to the world changed.

potentials of the new technology, Viola served the Everson Museum as a technical assistant, helping older established artists who were also in the early stages of exploring the video medium. This work provided an important basis for Viola's subsequent development.

Among the first artists Viola worked with was the Korean-born video pioneer Nam June Paik. Paik, a classically trained pianist and a serious student of history, language, and philosophy, pressed for a broader understanding of time as experienced within the Zen-derived notions of randomness and indeterminacy central to his personal Fluxus sensibility. Paik's outsider-insider experiences as a Korean public intellectual, first in postwar Japan and West Germany and then the United States, inspired a playful yet serious neo-Ludditism, a relentless deconstruction of Western modernist practices, a prescient understanding of cultural hybridity, and a Brechtian concern for interactivity in technologically based art.[5] Yet Paik's penchant for using technology to subvert the idea of technology manifests his stubborn insistence upon an art made for our own era. "Not cybernetic art," Paik noted, "but rather art for cybernetic times."[6]

It has been over a quarter century since Nam June Paik shocked the art world with his synthesized video and prepared television works. For many reasons, commercial television was an important target of Paik's Fluxus cultural insurgency.[7] But what Viola absorbed was Paik's irreverent respect for technology itself.

The contest between conflicting notions of culture and nature was quite prominent in Frank Gillette's video installations. Gillette's use of video to map natural systems and develop an alternative approach to landscape as subject is rooted in the crisis in sculptural practice precipitated by, among other things, the need to incorporate notions of epochal time into the representation of nature seen from a systemic, ecological perspective. In the late sixties and early seventies, Gillette created delicate and elegant video installations based on the direct observation of nature. Using the real-time capacity of videotape playback and freely mixing live video signals with prerecorded imagery, Gillette constructed multiple-channel video environments, such as *Tetragrammaton* (1972), in which one experienced time strangely unfixed from a single point of

---

5.   Bertolt Brecht's 1929 essay concerning his theory of radio spoke directly to the aesthetic and ideological roots of radio as a one-way medium. In many ways, this essay can be seen as the first manifesto of interactive media art, though Brecht's concern was the way in which one-way radio supported the growth of state fascism. See "The Radio as an Apparatus of Communication," in John G. Hanhardt, ed., *Video Culture: A Critical Investigation* (Layton, Utah: Gibbs M. Smith, Peregrine Smith Books, in association with the Visual Studies Workshop Press, 1986) pp. 53–55.

6.   Paik expressed the relationship between "cybernated art" and "cybernated life" with the following formula: $\int_{t=you}^{me} (\text{cybernated art}) \, dt - \frac{\text{art for cybernated life}}{dx} = \mid\frac{3}{\infty}\mid$

See Judson Rosebush, ed., *Nam June Paik, Videa 'n' Videology 1959–1973*, exh. cat. (Syracuse: Everson Museum of Art, 1974).

non-Cartesian spatial reference. Gillette's densely edited multiple-monitor installations and live video installations expanded the idea of temporal constructions within the video medium, combining an almost painterly collage sensibility with an intense literary predisposition to produce new ways of mapping experience of the real.

Working in a similar fashion, but from a radically different perspective, the Chilean sculptor and architect Juan Downey created precisely edited multiple-monitor installations to explore Magic Realist-inspired notions of relationships between the natural world and the man-made environment. Downey's focus, however, was on the idea of communication and energy structures—what he termed "invisible architecture." Producing video documents based on firsthand observation of peoples and ancient ritual sites in Central and South America, Downey sought a union between the idea of human communication and romanticized spiritual states. With roots in the fictions of Jorge Luis Borges and Thomas Kuhn's *The Structure of Scientific Revolutions,* Downey's tapes and video installations expanded the idea of ethnographic video

work by embedding a broadly defined concept of documentary video into a poetic and deeply personalized framework. His work, like that of his contemporaries Gordon Matta-Clark and Robert Smithson, insisted on the recognition of social concerns within the linked fields of archaeology and architecture-informed sculpture, and honored the intelligence of non-Western, often pre-industrial cultures.

Peter Campus, a major first-generation video artist, explored psychological aspects of perception. His installation work dealt powerfully with issues of the real—of self-awareness and self-reflection. By immersing the viewer in total room-scaled projected video environments, Campus forced a consideration of the physiology of perception as well as the psychological dimension of observation. His rigorous black-and-white, live interactive projections, such as *Negative Crossing* (1974), had an enormous influence, significantly expanding the aesthetic potential of the video image. Creating an intensely controlled sculptural space, Campus' mirroring spaces related physical appearance to representations of subtle psychological phenomena.

7. In a story often told by Paik, he chose video because he was a poor man from a poor country and had to chose a medium no one else was interested in. The strained humility aside, it was also Paik who brought sex to classical music by composing the famous topless cello performance for his collaborator Charlotte Moorman.

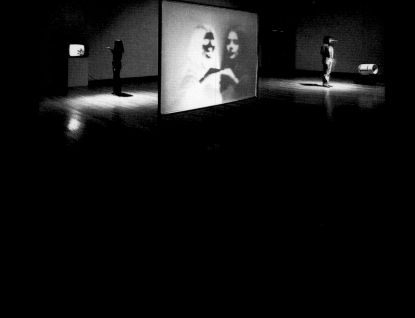

Peter Campus
Negative Crossing, 1974
As installed at the Everson Museum of Art

Perhaps only Bruce Nauman's early video work, such as that shown in his 1973 Whitney survey exhibition, was more profoundly influential for Viola and other artists who were exploring the territory of psychologically oriented, sculptural video environments. Nauman exhibited a deep understanding of the phenomenological function of video's real-time mirroring capacity, but unlike Campus' projected environments, Nauman's video work implied the possibility of spaces that exist only within the framework of a sculptural proposition. In this regard, his tough, Postminimal installations such as *Corridor Installation (Nick Wilder Installation)* (1970) were and remain paradigmatic. They are predicated on the idea that a viewer can be confronted with an image which can unsettle basic assumptions of one's body occupying a given space—an idea that emerged from Nauman's relation to the then-flourishing dance and performance sensibilities which were deeply influencing the sculptural activities of a generation. [8]

In an era of extreme skepticism, the real was what you could touch, bump into, count, name, see (and record). Or was that notion of the real too limiting? Too constrained by language and convention? Had art become too bound up in what deconstructionist critics saw as uneasy relationships between conflicting signifying structures and the contested goals of symbolic signification itself? Nauman's concrete actions begged questions about the structure that functions beneath language, in advance of conscious thought. Yet he sought to connect this philosophic inquiry to the physical world of direct experience.

These artists, with disparate goals and distinct working attitudes, demonstrate the broad range of approaches to video in circulation in the early 1970s. A unifying concern—the representation of real-world conditions—was approached from a variety of perspectives, but always with the intent to provoke a direct experience of the world. And this world was "real-time," endowed with the unique temporal character deeply identified with the live video image.

Viola took off from this convergence of influences in the early 1970s and developed a vocabulary and approach to video that quickly estab-

8. See Marcia Tucker's essay in *Bruce Nauman*, exh. cat. (Los Angeles: Los Angeles County Museum of Art; New York: Whitney Museum of American Art, 1972), pp. 31–49. In particular, see her comments on Nauman's relationship to Meredith Monk, p. 35.

lished his presence. He brought to his work the distilled attitudes of a socially and intellectually activist generation. Through personal, nearly diaristic writings and a consistent vision, he has created and nurtured a unique intellectual and spiritual foundation for his work. The work functions as an extension of direct personal observation of the everyday, presented as poetic intimations of the sublime in everyday life. Viola's notebooks reveal the evolution of an artist's working process and trace the ways in which his wide-ranging curiosity has powered a deep personal search for the sublime in both written and visual form. Viola's work achieves its distinction not only through its tone, but also from the particular character of his intellect and his artistic intentions. Rather than offer sardonic musings on cultural diversity, the power of signifying structures, or the force of social dissolution, Viola relies on craft, clarity, and a vision of the real that springs from beneath the visible surface of observable phenomena. Clearly at odds with the cynicism of his age, his work is informed by a set of spiritual values that has had a profound continuing impact on his development. Oddly enough, though life and death have often been his subject, his concern is not loss, but rather the sublime and the possibility of spiritual transcendence.

Viola's particular spirituality involves the open embrace and continuing study of non-Western art, music, and religion, which in part originated in a chance encounter with a Sufi-inspired artist and storyteller whom Viola met while working in Florence. [9] By associating Viola with historical artists working within sacred traditions, we sense his concern with the representation of the sublime and the evocation of transcendent states. It is a secular and intellectual concern, emerging not so much from religious training but from a different kind of conviction. For Viola, art's highest purpose and function is to be found within the profound tradition of "gift-giving," in the words of contemporary author-poet Lewis Hyde. [10] Viola does not discount the role of the work of art, or relegate it to a secondary status, but just the opposite: he elevates the creative act by insisting on its deeper social and spiritual function.

At the same time, Viola's art is not self-serious and is anything but dour. There is a humorous undercurrent influenced in equal parts by his continued study of the wondrous refined poetry and wit of the thirteenth-century Persian mystic and poet known as Rumi. But Viola also came of age in a time strongly influenced by the strange and irreverent

9.   See the conversation between Lewis Hyde and Bill Viola in this volume, p. 144.

10.   See Lewis Hyde, *The Gift: Imagination and the Erotic Life of Property* (New York: Random House, 1983).

Andrei Tarkovsky
From *Nostalgia*, 1983
Film, color and black-and-white; 125 minutes
Opera Film Productions for RAI-2, Italy; Sovin Film, Moscow

humor of Bob and Ray, the Firesign Theater, and Monty Python. From these comics, Viola absorbed a strong sense of the profoundly foolish. They also helped reinforce his already healthy sense of the absurd. Yet in Viola's work there is not much irony—the postmodern hallmark. If there is any at all, it is the residual irony of an artist who found himself drawn to work in a field unbounded by notions of tradition and critical dogma, only to emerge twenty-five years later deeply enmeshed in a series of intersecting spiritual traditions, both Western and Eastern, ancient and contemporary.

Viola's transparent use of the video apparatus is masterly: he has transformed the now omnipresent video technology into a medium capable of presenting images of extraordinary subtlety. We perceive his complex understanding of time (and timing), his absolute control of the video image itself, his singularly inventive understanding of sound, and of course his Zen-like use of the unexpected. These characteristics are indeed impressive, but in actual fact they only define the surface quality of the work.

Seeing one or two works in a group exhibition has an effect quite differ-

ent from seeing a larger body of work, such as that in Viola's "Buried Secrets" exhibition at the US Pavilion at the 1995 Venice Biennale. When video installations are linked as an integrated meta-work, deeper interconnections emerge, much like the difference between the composition of an individual song and the construction of a symphony. Both forms contain similar elements, but the epic quality of the larger work demands another level of control on the part of the artist and another level of engagement on the part of the viewer. The experience of Viola's installations is immersive—closer to that of floating under water than to watching a film. [11]

This ability to construct large-scale experiences through linked video installations is one Viola has developed further in recent years. The success of such works derives from his insistence on maintaining a simple and direct approach. Through video and computer-editing technology, he transforms direct observations into complex yet seamless constructions. Reliant upon a straightforwardness that masks its intricately crafted interior, these video constructions form the core of the larger works. Painstaking craft is evident, but it never gets in the way,

11.   The underwater music performance works of Max Neuhaus are close analogies here. In his underwater concerts, the audience floated in a large swimming pool heated to body temperature and listened to sound produced by water being pumped through a succession of thin plastic tubes through minia-

ture plastic whistles. The water whistles made a sound audible only to ears under the water's surface, and the experience of the random water whistle music was literally one of complete immersion in a fully ethereal sound space.

Jacopo Pontormo
Visitation, c. 1528-29
Oil on panel, 80 x 61" (202 x 156 cm)
Pieve di San Michele, Carmignano, Italy

never announces itself, being always in motion toward transparency.

Viola's approach couples his uncommon empathy with the viewer's conscious experience and a deep scientific understanding of the neurophysiological mechanisms of perception. As noted earlier, Viola inherited these concerns in large part from Peter Campus. The powerful intellectual and corporeal impact of Campus' video installations encouraged Viola's interest in the raw physicality of perception and cognition. Yet even in his earliest videotaped works, produced while still in art school, it was quite evident that Viola had a strong interest in the connections between the science of cognition and the metaphysical implications of consciousness.[12]

In early works such as *He Weeps for You* (1976), these concerns would be expressed primarily in terms of scientific methodology. However, in later works such as *The Crossing* (1996), they are explored more within metaphysical realms. In terms of an image vocabulary, Viola's preoccupation with water and fire, his profoundly moving meditations on birth and dying, his recurring use of extreme slow motion to create

states of altered consciousness—metaphorically evoked or directly represented in what we might term suspended time—locates him within a set of specific critical references.

These references are not to the historical practices of Surrealism or its associated intellectual connections to contemporary Freudian theory. Viola is resolutely a realist, though one who has found a space for his own approach to the real wedged somewhere between modernist concerns for art as a reflection of our collective unconscious and postmodern critiques of the sources and uses of dream and fantasy. He can be situated with other late twentieth-century artists who employ the symbolic codes drawn from sources as disparate as the great Georgian filmmaker Andrei Tarkovsky[13] and the works of the sixteenth-century Italian Mannerist Jacopo Pontormo, whose *Visitation* is the specific source of Viola's *The Greeting* (1995).[14]

Perhaps equally important, Viola developed an understanding of the ways contemporary art employed the structure and intelligence of traditional and non-Western art. In a recent conversation with me, he

12. Viola's student experience at Syracuse University had a strong influence. Not only did the art school support his early exploration of video as a creative medium, but the university's psychology department maintained a sophisticated laboratory for the study of sensory perception. Viola often availed himself, as an uninvited visitor, of the laboratory and its resources.

13. See J. Hoberman's essay in Barbara London, ed., *Bill Viola: Installations and Videotapes*, exh. cat. (New York: The Museum of Modern Art, 1987) pp. 63–72.

14. For Viola's use of Pontormo's *Visitation*, see Susie Kalil, "Buried Secrets," in Marilyn A. Zeitlin, *Bill Viola: Buried Secrets/Vergrabene Geheimnisse*, exh. cat. (Tempe, Arizona: Arizona State University Art Museum; Hannover, Germany: Kestner-Gesellschaft, 1995), p. 23.

Bill Viola
From *The Greeting*, 1995
Video/sound installation, 14' x 21'6" x 25'6" (4.3 x 6.6 x 7.8 m)
Artist's proof 2: Whitney Museum of American Art, New York;
Partial and promised gift of an anonymous donor P.4.95

observed that Buddhist works of art still function as sites of ritual offerings and prayer even when situated and recontextualized within Japanese art museums, outside their original temple settings. [15] Similarly, Viola has commented on the power and use of art, citing the famed sixteenth-century Isenheim Altarpiece by Matthias Grünewald, which was originally used as an integral part of a healing procedure. The different panels were opened and closed in a process that required the patient-viewer to spend hours in front of the altarpiece in prayer and contemplation. Does this work still function in the same way in a secularized museum context? Can art still fulfill an analogous role in our times? If so, should it? These are some of the questions implicit in Viola's demanding art. And his use of the installation form (especially when sited outside the art museum context) functions as an implied critique of the leveling and neutralizing function that the modern art museum inadvertently performs.

Viola nevertheless eschews overtly theoretical postmodern concerns: he does not question his role as an artist or provoke such questions in the minds of those experiencing his work. In the tradi-

tional manner of great art, Viola provokes the heart by leading the mind to avenues of contemplation and self-discovery. In so doing, the art provides the basis for an experience best described as transcendent—a curious word to use at the end of the age of mechanical reproduction, yet the only word that applies.

How does all this come about, given that lucid, straightforward, and precise observation of the sensate world lies at the core of Viola's working method? How we see and hear, how the brain processes what the eyes behold and the ears receive, as well as the mechanics of cognition are the stuff of Viola's work. This seems to place him in the context of artists allied to the spectacular intersection of art and technology. But Viola does not fit into that particular genre of postwar art, which is primarily concerned with the humanizing of technology and the essentialist critique of science as the root of the bankrupt philosophies of modernity.

If anything, Viola is a postmodern humanist: a humanist transformed by a lifelong devotion to Eastern spiritual thought, and a postmodern completely uninterested in the collapse of meaning. Viola's humanist skepti-

Bill Viola
From *He Weeps for You*, 1976
Video/sound installation, 12 x 26 x 36' (3.7 x 7.9 x 11 m)
Edition 2: Collection of Pamela and Richard Kramlich; courtesy Thea Westreich Art
Advisory Services

cism, which rejects critical dogma and theoretical doctrine, is best understood in terms of the writings of Rumi, who urged his students to delve beneath the many forms of surface appearance in the world and to avoid the distraction of scholarly theory. In a lecture delivered in 1988, Viola quotes Rumi: "This talk is like stamping new coins. They pile up,/while the real work is done outside/by someone digging in the ground."[16] Elsewhere, Rumi states, "You have seen the kettle of thought boiling over, now consider the fire!"[17] Yet Viola does not merely seek an understanding of consciousness, but rather he explores the daunting possibility of transforming it. His art does not rely on traditional religious faith, yet paradoxically it is fueled by an absolute belief in the transformative power of art and in a common human spiritual nature.

Again, in works such as *He Weeps for You*, Viola expressed his interest in the physics of perception as well as the metaphoric power of the direct act of looking and recognizing one's self as the subject of the work. Stepping into a spotlit circle within a darkened space, you are surprised by your projected video image, upside down and slowly stretching. In the time it takes to orient yourself to the source of the image, you notice that your image is gradually stretching into an elongated shape. It soon becomes apparent that the image we see is our refracted image contained within a tiny droplet of water, slowly forming from a brass valve at the end of a copper pipe. It also quickly dawns on us that the surface of the ballooning drop will eventually burst or the drop will fall from the miniature spigot. In time, the drop does fall, and it hits the amplified skin of a drum, producing a loud resonant sound. The sound-slap jars us out of our narcissistic reverie and returns us to the process, which immediately begins anew as the next drop forms and our seedling-image is once again attached to the water's subtly pulsing skin.

It is a video koan, instantly forming an indelible memory. It also redefines our idea of portraiture (self or other) by asserting a change in the ground rules for the representation of the individual by shifting the focus to the construction of a theater of concentrated self-awareness. Though time is not slowed down in this work—the process occurs in real time—we sense the density of time and its relative nature in relation to the level of our awareness. But perhaps most important to our understanding of Viola's work as a whole is that we emerge from the

16. From "Someone Digging in the Ground," in *The Essential Rumi,* trans. Coleman Barks (New York and San Francisco: Harper Collins Publishers, 1995), p.107.

17. Rumi, quoted by Viola in Robert Violette, ed., in collaboration with Bill Viola, *Reasons for Knocking at an Empty House: Writings 1973–1994* (Cambridge, Massachusetts: The MIT Press; London: Thames and Hudson, in association with Anthony d'Offay Gallery, 1995), p. 172.

experience of *He Weeps for You* literally changed. Recognizing a drop of water as both a lens and a metaphoric mirror alters our awareness of our place in the world and our relationship to time and materiality.

Though one may experience Viola's work in a social context typified by the museum gallery, the work itself retains a profoundly private character. Not unlike complex music, these time-based works insist on a concentrated focus. And because they refuse to describe the world in any recognizable documentary fashion, they can only succeed in constructing a model of space defined by memory and acute self-awareness. The work, however, is neither about nor reliant on self-consciousness, with its attendant implications of petty self-centeredness. Rather, the artist points to transcendent self-awareness, implying nothing less than the considered life made manifest within a work of art.

In work after work, from his ongoing series of room-scaled video installations to single-channel videos made to be seen within a context as alien to the aims of art as broadcast television, Viola evokes acutely realized simple truths about the human condition. The viewer soon comes to recognize the extensive range of the artist's concerns: the mysteries of birth and death; the relationship between consciousness, conscience, and memory; our foolish attempts to measure things of real value; the collapse of our notion of time; the possibility of transcendence and the power of grace.

The purpose of this exhibition and catalogue, then, is to allow Viola's richly interconnected oeuvre to be experienced as a complex new whole. The relationships that connect the artist's works to one another, and in fact resonate to create a larger composite installation, can only be fully experienced in this fashion. The careful disposition of these interrelated installations within and outside the museum provides not only ground for an overview of Viola's achievement, but literally constructs the scale and context necessary to step back far enough, so to speak, in order to fully comprehend the work for the first time.

Finally, when we're done looking and thinking, we return to the world to find that we've never left it at all. In fact, we've been deeply in the world of the real all the while, engaged in our feeling for the things themselves.

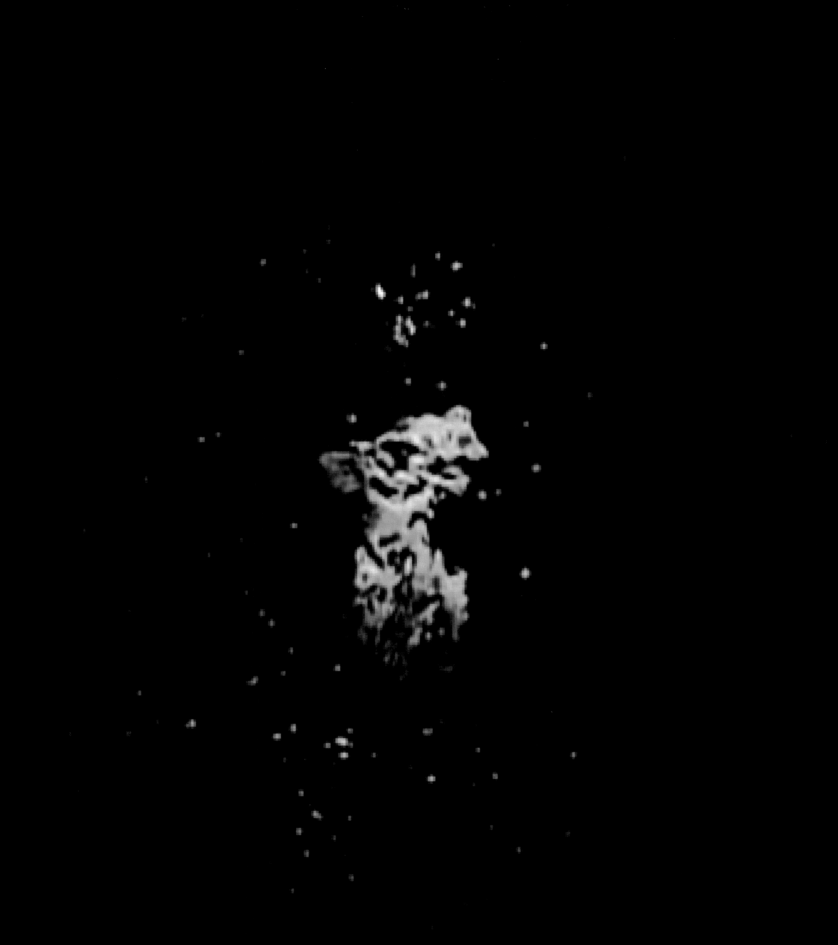

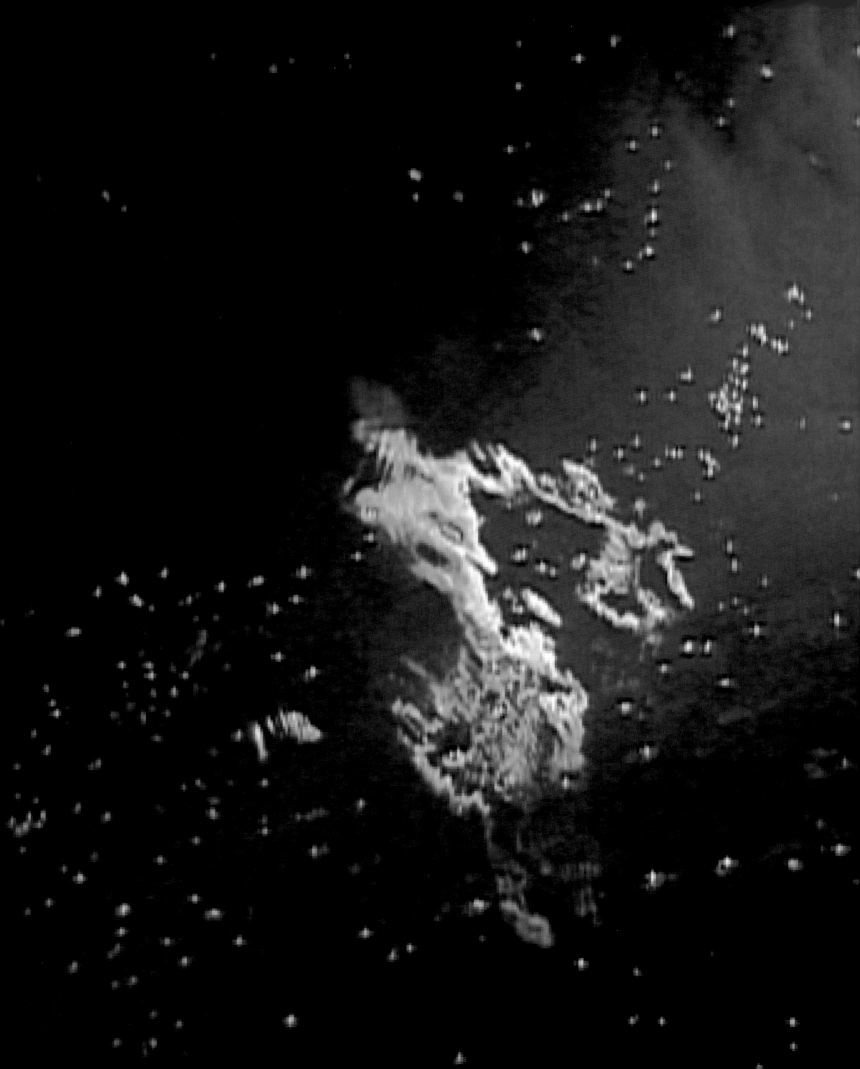

Selected Works: 1972–1996

Kira Perov and Bill Viola

Texts: Bill Viola

An attempt to stare down the self. A camera, with its live image displayed on a monitor next to it, is seen viewing its own reflection in a mirror when a man enters the room. He sits in front of the mirror, breaking the line of sight and thus becoming both the subject and the object of a self-portrait. He stares into the lens, maintaining eye contact and focused concentration with the unseen viewer. A low howling sound is heard, the noise of the camera's microphone in low-level feedback with its own speaker. The man stares at us for a long time. Suddenly, without warning, he bursts out with a loud violent scream. He then gets up and physically stops the videotape in the recorder with his hand, creating a violent disruption of picture and sound that plunges the screen into snow.

2

Composition "D"

1973

Videotape

An attempt to reach the fundamental state of the video signal through a system-
atic degeneration of the recording process. A view of a hallway is seen. A man
appears and, after moving an obstacle out of the way, he approaches, walking
toward the camera. He raises his hand and coughs just before leaving the
frame. This recorded action was then rerecorded and appears repeated at a
slower speed, lowering the pitch of the sound and degenerating the image
slightly. In turn, this slowed action was again rerecorded and reappears slowed
even further, eventuating in a series of repetitions whereby the image and
sound are progressively slowed and deteriorated. Finally, at the slowest speed,
the last frameline slips by and the image stops as a still picture, with the original image of the man and the hallway degenerated beyond recognition, sustained only as a memory in the viewer's mind.

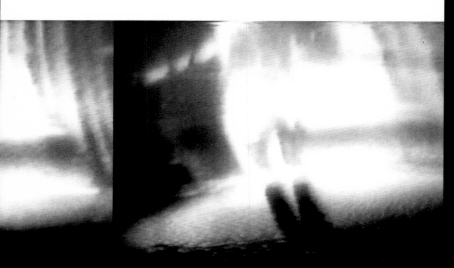

A common level is physically attached to the video camera by a special construction that links both to a single shared frame of reference. This physical construction is never seen directly, but creates a situation whereby everywhere the camera turns, in whatever orientation, the level is always visible at the bottom of the picture. An unseen cameraperson awkwardly maneuvers this cumbersome contraption from its original resting place in his house and out onto the street, in an exploration of his immediate neighborhood, at one point barely squeezing down a long narrow alley. All the while, the level remains a static visual fixture in the camera's field of view, futilely trying to fulfill its function in a constantly moving world, and calling attention to the relativity of all measuring devices, including the video camera itself.

4   Cycles

1973

Videotape

A large window fan is used to interrupt the scanning process of a broadcast TV image, challenging television's one-way dominance by pitting one domestic household device against another. The fan becomes a metaphor for the process of "blowing" information out from the screen and onto the viewer. At the same time, the varying speeds of the fan blades create optical interference patterns across the image that shift in stability as the fan speed comes in and out of phase with the fixed rate of the scanning TV picture. The fan alternately masks and reveals select frames of television, and simultaneously demonstrates the illusory nature of the image as a beam of rapidly scanning light.

Two sequences of distortions, one human and physical, the other electronic and visual, are presented in succession. First, a man's face is seen in close-up as he undergoes a series of violent contortions caused by physically pressing his face against a pane of glass positioned between himself and the camera. At times painful, at times comical, the facial contortions are presented within a pattern of edits, reordered and occasionally punctuated by a still frame. The abstract sound of electronic noise and distortion is heard throughout. The source of the sound is revealed in the next scene, in which a black-and-white video monitor placed on a table undergoes a series of electronic distortions that progressively disrupt the screen with unstable patterns of visual noise. The corresponding sonic distortions are audible from the monitor's speaker.

Information

1973

Videotape

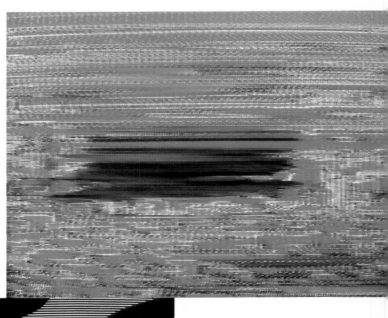

Information is the manifestation of an aberrant electronic nonsignal passing through the video switcher in a normal color TV studio, and being retrieved at various points along its path. It is the result of a technical mistake made while working in the studio late one night. The output of a videotape recorder was accidentally routed through the studio switcher and back into its own input. When the record button was pressed, the machine tried to record itself. The resulting electronic perturbations affected everything else in the studio. Color appeared where there was no color signal, there was sound where there was no audio connected, and every button pushed on the video switcher created a different effect. After this error was discovered and traced back, it became possible to sit at the switcher as if it were a musical instrument and learn to "play" this nonsignal. Once the basic parameters were understood, a second videotape recorder was used to record the result. *Information* is that tape.

6

The Mysterious Virtue

1974

Installation

A pile of river-worn stones is placed on a woven mat on the floor. A high-intensity lamp illuminates them in a bright pool of focused light. Two loudspeakers face the mat from opposite directions. A strong low vibration is heard, the sound of two separate sine waves tuned to a frequency of approximately fifty cycles per second, near the lower threshold of human hearing. A slight difference in tuning between the two frequencies causes the sound waves to beat against each other in the space, audible as a regularized shifting or slow oscillation of the standing wave patterns of sound in the room. The sine wave is a pure waveform of nature, present acoustically in sound and visibly in the movement of water. The slowly undulating wave patterns of low-frequency sound, themselves invisible physical forms, "wash" over the rocks and spill out into the room, recapitulating the motion of the water waves that originally wore down the rough surfaces of the stones, transforming them imperceptibly over time into the smooth rounded forms of their present state.

8

Bank Image Bank

1974

Video installation

A reformulation of the video closed-circuit surveillance system into an interactive sculpture that reconfigures the viewer's experience of space and, in the process, alters the perception of the individual's self-image. Two opposing banks of six monitors each display live inputs from eight black-and-white closed-circuit video cameras. The monitors are stacked two high by three wide in two configurations that face each other from across a distance of 30 feet, with the viewer able to walk between them.

The two central monitors in each bank form the focal point of the piece. On bank 1, these monitors display the images from two cameras mounted on automatic scanning motors, one rightside up, the other upside down. The viewer then sees two images of his or her own body alternately moving

into and out of itself as determined by the vertical scanning motion of the cameras. On bank 2, the central monitors display camera views of the two escalators in the bank's lobby. Here, the vertical motion of merger and separation seen on bank 1 is repeated by the vertical positioning of the cameras, which show passersby on the up and down escalators repeatedly merging into one another, or, during quiet times, disappearing into an imaginary vanishing point between the screens.

Four other stationary cameras, two on each side, are aimed at a close-up of the monitor screens on the opposite image bank, creating visual feedback loops that result in the appearance of screens within screens on all the monitors in the system. As viewers step between the banks of monitors, they see themselves standing in the space, simultaneously visible from both front and back, normal and left-to-right reversed, rightside up and upside down, electronically mirrored in infinite reflections, and vertically scanning in and out of themselves, all while seeing other images of people on nearby escalators who are undergoing similar transformations within the system.

9

Instant Breakfast

1974
Videotape

Instant Breakfast was videotaped in a darkened studio with an electronic photoflash providing the only sufficient light source for the video camera. Presented are a succession of images of the moment of impact of violent acts of destruction, visible only as discrete individual video frames revealed by the photoflash. The images occur in the space of an eyeblink and are perceived as momentary afterimages on both the video camera tube and the viewer's retina, becoming extended in time only through memory. For the majority of the time we are in blackness, and the sound becomes the dominant unifying element and link to the imagination.

10

Olfaction

1974
Videotape

Five discrete actions occurred in the same space and were record-ed from a single fixed camera. These recordings were superim-posed to create a composite space where all activity merges into an artificial "present," and the apparent solidity of objects is directly dependent on their previ-ous existence in time. The video-tape is based on the functioning of the sense of smell, a sensory modality strongly linked to memo-ry and designed to integrate infor-mation about past events into the present moment.

A Million Other Things (2)

1975
Videotape

Changes in light and sound on the edge of a pond during an eight-hour period, from afternoon to night, are composed into rhythmic variations resembling music. The individual is seen as a static fixture in the environment, sitting immobile in a chair for the duration. Finally, the sun sets, and he remains the sole visible object illuminated by a single electric lamp.

12

Return

1975
Videotape

The composition of the tape reflects the sonic structure of a ringing bell, complete with its echoes and subsequent reverberations. A man is seen within a natural landscape, moving toward the camera while pausing every few steps to ring a brass bell he is carrying in his hand. As the tape progresses, each time the bell is struck, a rapid edit sequence carries the figure back through each previous position where the bell was rung, all occurring within the time of the fading sound of a single ring. As the man advances, a cumulative process occurs whereby at each station his image is momentarily thrust back to the starting point, only then to advance further. Finally reaching his destination, he arrives at the camera, where his body momentarily blocks the view. He then is taken through all the stages of the journey in a single instant, returning to the point from where he began.

13   Il Vapore

1975
Video/sound installation

In a small, raised alcove at the back of a large empty room, eucalyptus leaves are boiling in a metal pot of water. The area is spotlit, and the vapor can be seen rising into the air. The strong smell of eucalyptus permeates the room. The pot is resting on a straw mat. Behind this, at the rear of the alcove, is a black-and-white monitor with a video camera, and a spotlight high on the wall. The camera is focused on the area around the metal pot, with some of the larger room behind it in view. The live image of the boiling pot is mixed with a videotape made from the same camera at a previous time. This is visible on the monitor screen. The videotape is of a man kneeling behind the pot, slowly transferring water from a bucket to the pot with his mouth, gradually filling it over a period of one hour. The sound of the water pouring can be heard from a small loudspeaker. Viewers entering the space witness the empty alcove with the pot of boiling water, while on the monitor they can see their own image coexisting with that of a person who appears to be kneeling at the pot in front of them. Both merge as ghostlike images inhabiting the present moment.

A collection of four visual "songs" in allegorical form, each independent yet linked rhythmically and conceptually into a larger whole. The video images and sounds were composed in a process similar to the composition of music, and function as visual allegories describing the psychological and emotional dynamics of the individual in interaction with the environment.

15

Songs of Innocence

1976

Videotape

Junkyard Levitation

Junkyard Levitation is a visual play on "mind over matter." Scrap metal technology and video technology are united to temporarily break down the known laws of science and to prove that psychokinesis, the ability to will physical objects to move, is valid in a given frame of reference.

1976

Videotape

Songs of Innocence is a reference to the work of William Blake. A group of children is seen singing a song on the lawn of a suburban parochial school. They walk off, leaving an object behind on the grass. The light undergoes a series of accelerated transformations as the sun begins to set. The images and voices of the children reappear at dusk, barely visible and audible as shadowy presences floating on the wind, engaging the viewer's perceptions and evoking a visual relationship between the transitions of memory, the setting of the sun, and death. A culminating camera zoom into the object left behind reveals it to be a vase with flowers and a small eternal flame.

The structure of *The Space Between the Teeth* is the structure of the acoustic phenomena and psychological dynamics of a person repeatedly screaming at the top of his lungs at the end of a long, dark industrial corridor. The camera point of view is made to travel down the length of the hallway and into the teeth of the person in proportionally accelerating increments within the space of each scream. Mathematically derived time relationships were applied using the then new computer-editing techniques to describe the acceleration and to articulate a foreground/background reversal, whereby a mundane domestic scene of a kitchen progressively appears in visual counterpoint to the screams. We are finally drawn to a close-up of a dripping water faucet, a momentary pause before a final transformation of disintegration and destruction where the world becomes image and is washed away on a wave.

17 Truth Through Mass Individuation

1976

Videotape

Truth Through Mass Individuation refers to Carl Jung's writings on the individual and the mass. The images and sounds of three abrupt and violent actions (a man leaping off a rock into a river, a flock of pigeons startled by a loud sound, a man firing a gun in a deserted city street) are seized and extended in time. Tension is regularly held, then released, as the figure is seen on the verge of frustrated aggression against the environment. In the fourth and final stage, he passively surrenders and walks off into the distance to be absorbed into the screaming mass of forty thousand people at a night baseball game.

He Weeps for You

1976

Video/sound installation

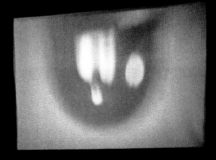

In a darkened space, a copper pipe runs down from the ceiling, terminating in a small brass valve, from which a single drop of water is slowly emerging. A live color video camera, fitted with a special lens attachment used for extreme close-up magnification, is focused in on this drop. The camera is connected to a video projector that displays the swelling drop of water on a large screen at the rear of the space. The optical properties of the waterdrop cause it to act like a wide-angle lens, revealing an image of the room and those within it. The drop grows in size gradually, swelling in surface tension, until it fills the screen. Suddenly it falls out of the picture and a loud, resonant sound is heard as it lands on an amplified drum. Then, in an endless cycle of repetition, a new drop begins to emerge and again fill the screen.

The simultaneous scales represented in the live video/water system draw a connection to the traditional philosophy or belief that everything on the higher order of existence reflects, and is contained in, the manifestation and operation of the lower orders. This idea has been expressed in ancient religious terms as the symbolic correspondence of the mundane (the earth) and the divine (the heavens), and is also represented in theories of contemporary physics that describe how each particle of matter in space contains knowledge or information of the entire system.

A large oak tree standing alone in an open field was spotlit by a high-powered searchlight beam positioned a quarter of a mile away. The searchlight was turned on in the late afternoon. As the daylight faded, the beam gradually became visible and the tree glowed with luminous intensity into the night. A negative shadow of its dark form was cast out across the valley, visible for several miles. The moon was also seen at times coming through the clouds behind the tree. The beam was turned off several hours after the sun had set.

20

The Morning After the Night of Power

1977

Videotape

"The night of power" is described in the Koran as a moment when angels descend from the heavens to impart the divine inspiration. A static camera observes a still life of objects in a room with a large window. The light begins to change and soon it becomes apparent that a time-lapse view of the room is revealing variations in lighting conditions and times of day. The center of attention in the image is a ceramic vase sitting on a polished wood table, the vase positioned at the true center of the video frame. The objects on the table around the vase and throughout the room begin changing too, appearing and disappearing to reflect their shifting positions over the several days that the scene was originally observed. At times subtle, at other times dramatic, the still scene comes alive with the shifting movement of objects and light, continually drawing the viewer's gaze off the central static object until a final moment of great liberation, when a single camera movement transports the scene to another space while allowing the vase to remain unchanged.

Sweet Light

1977

Videotape

Various situations and image transformations are organized around the central theme of the phototropic vision of the moth and its relation to the ecstasy of self-annihilation. A moth emerges from a discarded letter as the spirit of a dead thought. The camera wildly circles an open candle flame on a table in a dizzying ecstatic dance. Frenzied moths fly above an intense light, out of view below the frame, the trails of their flight paths imprinting afterimages onto the camera tube against the night sky, with smoke rising from below as they plunge uncontrollably into the searing light. An individual appears in the distance, approaching through the moths' luminous tracings, and is inexorably drawn into the source of light and consumed.

Videotape collection

The Reflecting Pool is a collection of five independent works composed to function as a whole. Each uses varying styles and techniques to advance the theme of the collection: the progressive stages of the personal journey from birth to death, described through images of transition—from day to night, object to reflection, motion to stillness, time to timelessness.

22

The Reflecting Pool

1977–79

Videotape

A man emerges from the forest and stands before a pool of water. He leaps up and time suddenly stops. All movement and change in the otherwise still scene is limited to the reflections and undulations on the surface of the pond. Time becomes extended and punctuated by a series of events seen only as reflections in the water. The work describes the emergence of the individual into the natural world, a baptism into a world of virtual images and indirect perceptions.

An expression of the feminine principle. A woman stands indoors before a window in the city, silhouetted against the outside world as light and shadow shift, and day and night converge on her body. Still shadows within her form transform into a rushing waterfall sweeping over dark rocks with a violent motion and roaring sound, until stillness intervenes in the form of the serene interplay of light and shadow unfolding within a glass of water at dawn in the desert, the sun and the landscape refracted and contained in its rounded form.

24

Silent Life

1979

Videotape

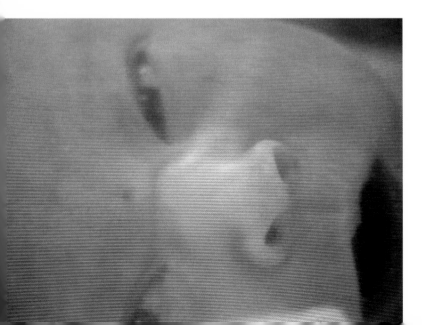

A document of the first images of life. A series of portraits of newborn babies from five minutes to one day old recorded in a hospital nursery. Newly formed conscious awareness flickers across the faces in a close-up view that reveals both the nature of institutional birth and the pure open being of individual newborn life.

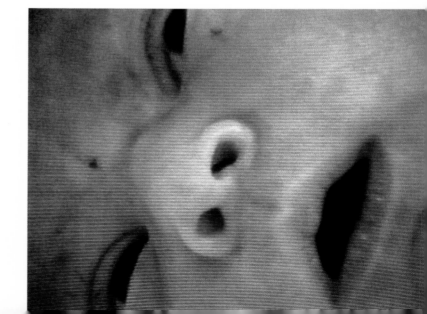

LIBRARY
UNIVERSITY OF ST. FRANCIS
JOLIET, ILLINOIS

25

Ancient of Days

1979–81

Videotape

A series of canons and fugues for video expressing the nature of the passage of time. Diverse rhythms of natural and subjective time are interwoven into a complex whole in a structure similar to music composition. Time becomes fluid to describe a world where destruction, run in reverse, becomes creation, where the larger patterns of changing weather on the face of a mountain unfold within the time of a fleeting human action, and the inexorable winding down of time cycles leads to a muted scene of a still life, where remaining natural change is confined within a picture frame hanging on the wall.

26

Vegetable Memory

1978–80

Videotape

A spiraling editing structure creates a kind of temporal magnifying glass to explore the phenomenon of repetitive cyclical viewing in the context of death and material dissolution. A repeating cycle of images of fish being processed at the Tsukiji fish market in Tokyo becomes progressively extended in time, greatly changing the form, feeling, and ultimately the meaning of the original shots as they move further into the domain of the subjective and the pictorial.

Chott el-Djerid (A Portrait in Light and Heat)

1979

Videotape

Chott el Djerid is the name of a vast, dry salt lake in the Tunisian Sahara Desert, where mirages are most likely to form in the midday sun. Here the intense desert heat manipulates, bends, and distorts the light rays to such an extent that you actually see things that are not there. Trees and sand dunes float off the ground, the edges of mountains and buildings ripple and vibrate, color and form blend into one shimmering dance. The desert mirages are set against images of the bleak winter prairies of Illinois and Saskatchewan, Canada, some of them recorded in a snowstorm. The opposite climactic conditions induce a similar aura of uncertainty, disorientation, and unfamiliarity.

Through special telephoto lenses adapted for video, the camera confronts the final barrier of the limits of the image, the point when the breakdown of normal conditions, or the lack of visual information, causes us to reevaluate our perceptions of reality and realize that we are looking at something out of the ordinary—a transformation of the physical into the psychological. If one believes that hallucinations are the manifestation of some chemical or biological imbalance in the brain, then mirages and desert heat distortions can be considered hallucinations of the landscape. It was like physically being inside someone else's dream.

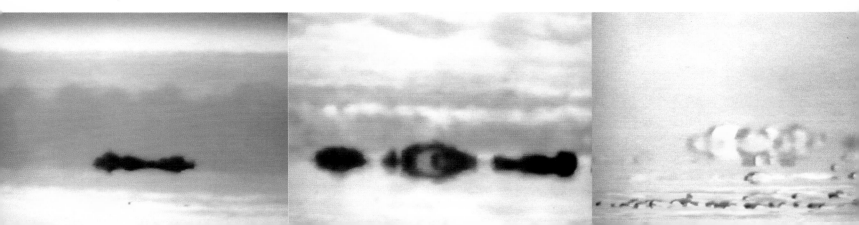

28   The Talking Drum

1979

Music composition

For Herman Heins

An improvisation for percussion and echoes in a resonant hall, with prerecorded sounds incorporated as low-level audible "shadows" within the reverberations. A large bass drum is beat repeatedly in a rhythmic pattern in a large resonant space. (The work was originally performed in an empty indoor swimming pool with an acoustic reverberation of over nine seconds.) The sequence of improvised drum beats moves between slow rhythmic patterns of discernible strokes to periods of rapid high intensity, where individual drumbeats merge into a larger mass of continuous noise. The highly resonant character of the space compounds this effect as the percussive beats begin to interact with their own echoes. The combination of the drumbeats and their architectural reflections creates a complex array of sound, as the reverberating waves continue to reinforce, cancel, and generally interfere with one other in the room.

After an exploration of these acoustic phenomena, the drumming again becomes sparse and simple, and prerecorded sounds are introduced from a single loudspeaker. Various natural sounds, such as dogs barking, people yelling, birds screeching, and machinery operating, are run through an electronic gate, a device that follows the loudness contours of an external sound, in this case the drumbeats. This allows these sounds to reach the speaker, and thus the room, only when the drum is struck. They fade out as the drumbeats die out in the space. However, the loudness of the drum at the moment when it is struck overpowers these sounds and momentarily masks them, so that they are only present in the room as sonic "afterimages," audible primarily within the time that the dying reverberations trail off in the space. At first, it is only apparent to listeners that the character of the echoes has changed, but then gradually they become aware of the new sounds contained within the individual drumbeats. The more the drum is beat, the more the shadow sounds are heard. The resonant characteristics of the architecture in turn affect the introduced sounds, altering their original qualities and sonic form. A second improvisational exploration of this new subtle and complex situation is then conducted by the performer.

29   Tunings from the Mountain

1980

Music composition

Tunings from the Mountain is the name of the music created to accompany a collaborative performance/event titled *Fog Sculpture*, directed by the Japanese artist Fujiko Nakaya and involving her created fog, a composition for laser light, and sound/music. An eight-channel string instrument was designed and constructed for the performance. It consisted of eight various weights of piano wire stretched over eight individual pieces of wood, each approximately 7 feet long. The strings were tuned in harmonic relationship within a single octave using built-in tuning pegs and movable bridges. Audio transducers (of the type used in David Tudor's *Rainforest*) were mounted at one end of each of the wood-frame boards, and prerecorded natural sounds were sent to them from eight individually amplified tape playback sources. The sounds consisted of recordings made in the local environment, as well as various natural sounds such as wind, birds, insects, running water, a squeaking swing set, motorized equipment in operation, dogs howling, and other animal sounds.

The transducers transmitted the sound sources into the wood of the instrument, thereby sending the strings into sympathetic vibration. Based on the piano wire weights and tensions, the playback sounds excited certain resonant frequencies in the strings, greatly transforming the sonic character of the original sounds. These vibrations were amplified by electromagnetic guitar pickups mounted to each wood frame. The sound of the individual strings was fed into a mixing board, where it was adjusted and equalized and then sent out to eight large loudspeakers. The loudspeakers were positioned throughout the landscape of a small river valley in the mountains near the town of Kawaji, Japan. In addition, microphones placed at the river's edge fed live water sounds to the instrument, and two parabolic reflectors with mounted speakers were used at times to sweep beams of sound across the environment. Finally, one of the members of a local *taiko* drumming group, which opened the performance, returned at the end of the piece to perform on the largest drum, the *odaiko*. His drumbeats were fed into all eight channels of the instrument simultaneously, becoming the last sound heard at the end of the performance.

SPEAKER PLACEMENT

DISTANCES (from Audio Control)
ADD 2-3 meters each
for excess, connections, etc.

1. 80 m
2. 55 m
3. 80 m
4. 80 m
5. 61 m
6. 80 m
7. 78 m
8. 70 m.

Hatsu-Yume (First Dream)

1981
Videotape

For Daien Tanaka

A visual journey of the camera eye through the landscape of Japan, from the rural areas of the far north, location of the "land of the dead" at Osorezan mountain, to the luminous nocturnal underworld of the streets of modern Tokyo. The work is structured on the cycle of one day, the dividing line of light and darkness, the ancient and the new, nature and city, object and subject, rational thought and unconscious insight.

Toward the end of the tape, after a purgation through light and color during a deluge from a violent rainstorm on a car windshield, fish appear as rippling gold and orange hues under the surface of the water. The disembodied consciousness of the roving camera finally takes root on the night streets of Tokyo when an individual emerges from the urban landscape to strike a match flame. Sweeping the glare of a bright light directly into the lens, he finally disappears into the night shadows of a bamboo forest, trailing the silver-purple thread of a fading afterimage on the camera tube, recalling the first rays of sunrise that pierced the darkness at the beginning of the work.

The piece unfolds in extended time as a visual trance about light and its relation to water and to life, and also to its opposite—darkness or the night and death. Here, video treats light like water—it becomes a fluid on the video tube. Water supports the fish like light supports man. Land is the death of the fish. Darkness is the death of man.

31   Reasons for Knocking at an Empty House

1982

Video/sound installation

At the end of a long, dark space, a heavy wooden chair sits spotlit before a TV monitor that shows a videotape of a man's face in close-up. He looks extremely tired, yet he stares intensely at the camera. Occasionally, a figure enters out of the background shadows and approaches the man from behind. He strikes the man violently over the head with a rolled-up magazine, and walks away.

This is what appears on the monitor. The room is silent and the chair empty. Stereo headphones mounted on the chair back invite visitors to sit down. Putting on the headphones, the viewer enters an inner stereo sound space. Every movement, every internal sound of the man on the screen is audible, even exaggerated—his breathing, swallowing. Voices and vague murmurings are barely heard beneath these sounds, whispering in continuous dialogue. The viewer merges with the internal space of the man, until the man is struck from behind and two speakers in the room suddenly emit a violent burst of extremely loud prerecorded sounds. The room immediately returns to silence, and the voices in the headphones begin again.

The installation is dedicated to the memory of Phineas P. Gage, who in 1848 suffered an accident while working on a Vermont railroad. A blast charge exploded prematurely and sent an iron bar through his left cheek and out of his forehead, leaving a large gaping hole where the front of his brain had been. Moments later, Gage was conscious and able to speak, and miraculously he soon recovered sufficiently to return to work. However, the former efficient and likable foreman had now become foul-mouthed and bad-tempered, obstinate and irresponsible. Unable to hold a job, he drifted around the country, eventually exhibiting himself and the iron bar as a sideshow attraction. His skull and iron bar are still on display in the museum of the Harvard Medical School.

32   Reasons for Knocking at an Empty House

1983

Videotape

An attempt to stay awake continuously for three days while confined to an upstairs room in an empty house. Recordings were made from a stationary black-and-white camera to chronicle the effects of the relentless passage of time on a solitary individual. The daylight changes. Cars pass by, visible from the windows. Sounds from the outside world enter the room. The man paces and changes position. He sips water; eats an apple. Day again turns to night. He struggles to stay awake. The space becomes increasingly subjective, both for the man and for the viewer, as events slide in and out of conscious awareness and duration becomes more and more brutal.

33

Room for St. John of the Cross

1983
Video/sound installation

A small black cubicle (6 x 5 x 5 ½ feet) stands in the center of a large dark room. There is a small open window in the front of the cubicle where a soft glow of incandescent light emerges. On the back wall of the space, a large screen shows a projected black-and-white video image of snow-covered mountains. Shot with an unstable hand-held camera, the mountains move in wild, jittery patterns. A loud roaring sound of wind and white noise saturates the room from two loudspeakers.

The interior of the cubicle is inaccessible and can be viewed only through the window. The inner walls are white. The floor is covered with brown dirt. There is a small wooden table in the corner with a metal water pitcher, a glass of water, and a 4-inch color monitor. On the monitor is a color image of a snow-covered mountain. Shot with a fixed camera, it is presented in real time with no editing. The only visible movement is caused by an occasional wind blowing through the trees and bushes. From within the cubicle, the sound of a voice softly reciting St. John's poems in Spanish is barely audible above the loud roaring of the wind in the room.

The Spanish poet and mystic St. John of the Cross (1542–1591) was kept prisoner by the religious establishment for nine months in 1577. His cell had no windows and he was unable to stand upright. He was frequently tortured. During this period, St. John wrote most of the poems for which he is known. His poems often speak of love, ecstasy, passage through the dark night, and flying over city walls and mountains.

A videotape of a living, beating human heart is played through a color monitor positioned over a large stainless-steel bowl of water. The glow of the video image is seen on the surface of the water. This configuration is situated at the central axis of the installation, which is laid out along a straight line. Behind the monitor at the far end-pole of the piece is a wooden antique end table. On top of the table is a small ceramic vase resting on a brass tray. Attached to the table by a wooden arm is a magnifying glass lens. A focused spotlight illuminates the vase. The lens is aligned at the precise optical focal point to project an inverted and slightly enlarged image of the vase onto a white screen suspended behind it.

An audio transducer concealed inside the table conducts the sound of the pounding heart to a long thin wire that stretches from the table to a large stone lying at the base of the installation 16 feet away. The stone serves to weight the wire to tension, and a continuous drone is produced by the open-tuned string. Two loudspeakers fill the room with its subtle and complex sound. The delicate physical vibrations of the wire embody the living, fragile nature of a dynamic system where all the elements are interdependent, animated by the energy (optical, electronic, and acoustic) transferred from the beating heart directly into the material components of the work.

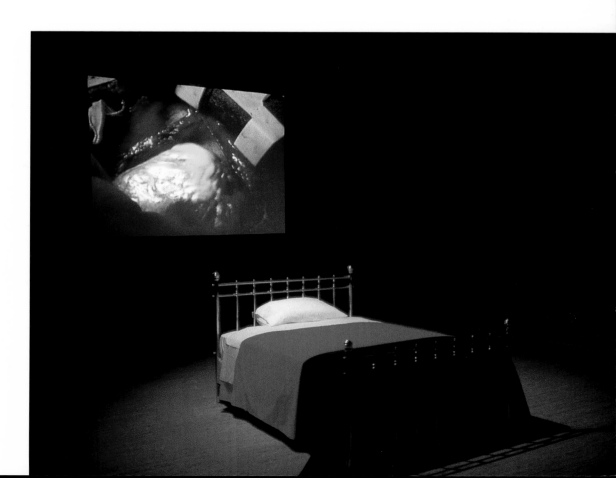

35   # Science of the Heart

1983

Video/sound installation

An empty brass bed sits in a large dark room. It is illuminated by a small overhead spotlight. A few feet behind the headboard, floating above in space, is a color video-projected image of a living, beating human heart. The sound of the pounding heart fills the room. The videotape of the heart beating has been manipulated in time so that it gradually speeds up to a high-pitched intensity of about twenty times normal speed, and then slows down through real time to extremely slow single beats, finally coming to rest in silence as a still image. After a long pause, the heart begins beating again and another cycle is initiated, continuing in endless repetition.

The common image of the bed contains deeper psychological references, simultaneously recalling birth, sex, sleep and dreaming, illness and death. The heart is an image of the rhythm of life—the human pulse, clock, and generator of the life force. Stillness can simultaneously be pre-birth and death. It is the transition from stillness to motion which recalls birth—the transition from motion to stillness which recalls death. The pattern of "crescendo-peak-decrescendo" is the basic rhythmic structure of life itself, and reflexively of many of our activities within it. The moment of peak intensity becomes the climax, the peak of life's actions or, as extreme physical exertion, the orgasm. The places between "beginning" and "ending" are subjectively determined by the viewer's entry into the space. The alternations of intensification and slowing are structured in a loop, and become only turning points along a larger, never-ending cycle of repetitions.

36   Anthem

1983
Videotape

Anthem originates in a single piercing scream emitted by an eleven-year-old girl standing in the reverberant hall of Union Railroad Station in Los Angeles. The original scream of a few seconds is extended and shifted in time to produce a primitive "scale" of seven harmonic notes, which constitute the soundtrack of the piece. Related in form and function to the religious chant, *Anthem* describes a contemporary ritual evocation centered on the broad theme of materialism—the architecture of heavy industry, the mechanics of the body, the leisure culture of Southern California, the technology of surgery, and their relation to our deep primal fears, darkness, and the separation of body and spirit.

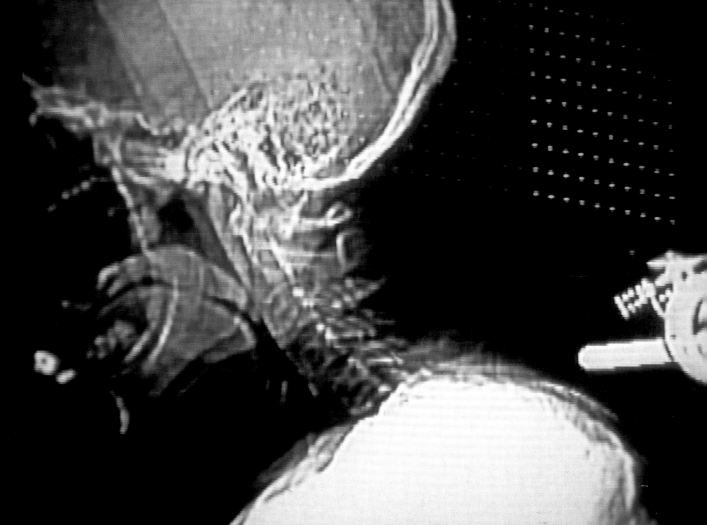

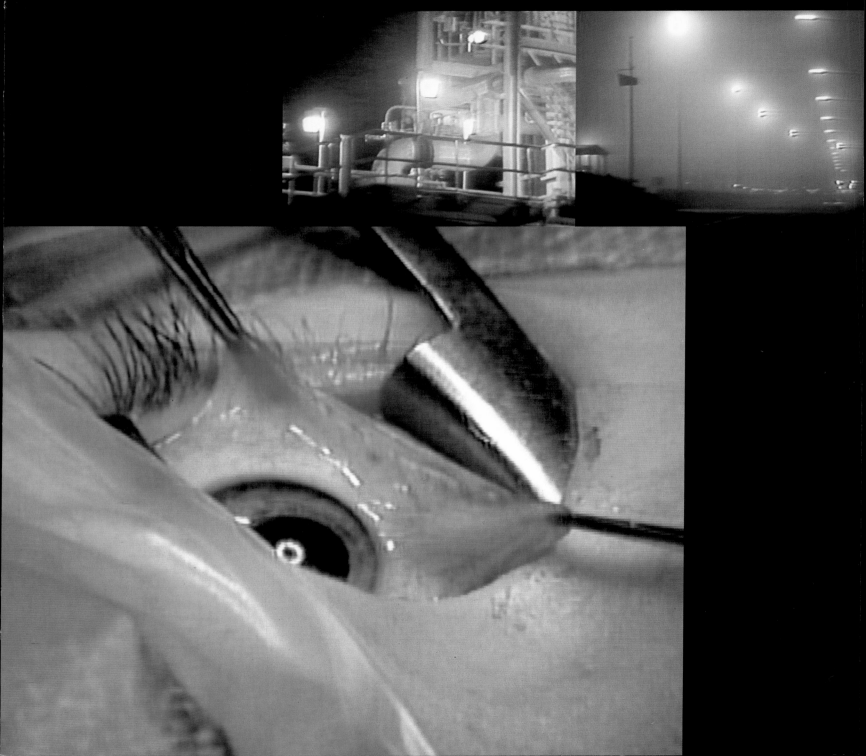

37 <h1>Reverse Television—Portraits of Viewers</h1>

1983
Broadcast television project

Reverse Television was conceived as a sculptural form to temporarily "puncture" the daily broadcast schedule, creating a series of momentary openings intended to reveal the hidden dimension of television—the silent, invisible presence of a multitude of viewers, behind and beneath all programs at every instant. Isolated from and oblivious to one another, they remain nameless in the anonymous privacy of their own homes.

A series of portraits was made of people sitting at home, staring in silence at the camera. Sound was recorded together with the picture. Forty-four portraits were made in the Boston area, with subjects ranging in age from sixteen to ninety-three years old. Ten continuous minutes were recorded with each person. An unbroken one-minute segment of this material was selected for broadcast. The portraits were to be shown each hour of the broadcast day as image inserts between programs. They would appear unannounced, with no titles before or after, and the series would run for several weeks. WGBH-TV Boston presented *Reverse Television* during a two-week period, November 14–28, 1983. They chose to air the portraits for thirty seconds each, showing them five times a day.

Later, a compilation tape was made that presents fifteen-second excerpts of all the portraits in the order they were recorded and represents a documentation of the project.

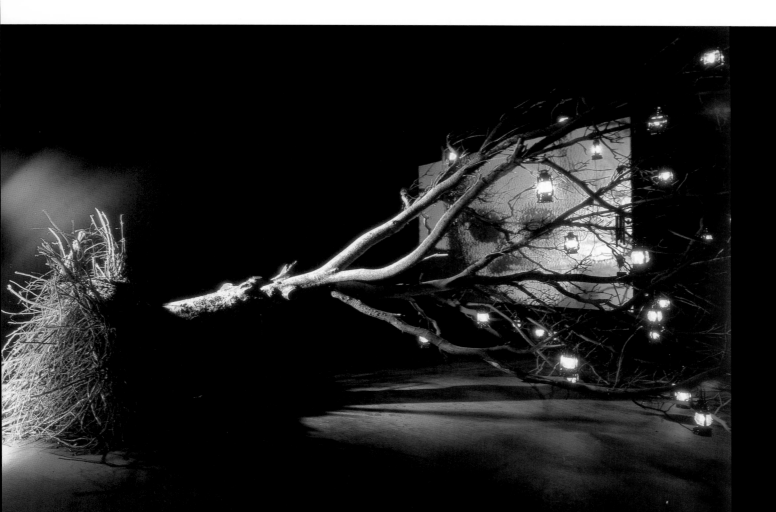

38   The Theater of Memory

1985

Video/sound installation

A large tree leans diagonally across the room, its exposed roots at the floor near the entrance, and its bare branches stretching to the ceiling at the far corner of the space. Fifty small electric lanterns are hung on its branches. Up on the rear wall is a large video-projected image. The picture is dominated by electronic noise and static patterns. Recognizable images are seen trying to break through, but they never come in clearly. Bursts of loud static and noise come through the speakers, as if a loud clear sound were about to come on, but never does. There are long silences between the bursts of noise. The only light in the room comes from the flickering lanterns and the violent flashing of the video image. The only continuous sound in the room is the delicate tone of a small wind chime hanging from a tree branch.

There has been much speculation, scientific and philosophical, on the causes and processes of the triggering of nerve firings in the brain that recreate patterns of past sensations, finally evoking a memory. Central to the brain's operation is the fact that all its neurons are physically disconnected from each other, and begin and end in a tiny gap of empty space. The flickering pattern evoked by the tiny sparks of thought bridging

39 I Do Not Know What It Is I Am Like

1986
Videotape

"When a man sought to know how he should live he went into solitude and cried until some animal brought wisdom to him."
—Letakots-Lesa, Pawnee Chief

I Do Not Know What It Is I Am Like is a personal investigation of the inner states and connections to animal consciousness we all carry within. The work is in five parts, and it functions like a map rather than a description of the animal psyche. Images of animals mediate a progression from an initial stage of nondifferentiation or "pure being" (a herd of bison moves within a vast open landscape, the camera confronts the glaring eye of an owl), proceeding through stages of the rational and the physical orders (a researcher is at work in his study, a dense montage of images flickers past at the limits of perception), finally arriving at a state beyond logic and the laws of physics (devotees in trance participate in a Hindu firewalking ritual, a fish is seen to fly out of a mountain lake, soaring over the tree tops to come to rest on the floor of a pine forest).

As the gateway to the soul, the pupil of the eye has long been a powerful symbolic image and evocative physical object in the search for knowledge of the self. The color of the pupil is black. It is on this black that you see your self-image when you try to look closely into your own eye, or into the eye of another—the largeness of your own image preventing you from having an unobstructed view within. It is the black we "see" when all the lights have been turned off, the space between the glowing electron lines of the video image, the space after the last cut of a film, or the luminous black of the nights of the new moon. It is through this black that we confront the gaze of an animal, partly with fear, with curiosity, with familiarity, with mystery. We see ourselves in its eyes while sensing the irreconcilable otherness of an intelligence ordered around a world we can share in body but not in mind.

A narrow corridor 20 feet long leads to a small inner room. One large wall of this room is actually a rear-projection screen displaying a moving image, floor to ceiling, wall to wall, 16 feet wide by 12 feet high. A videotape of a four-year-old's birthday party is playing back at $1/16$ normal speed. Sounds and images fill the room as the original twenty-six-minute videotape now takes approximately seven hours to unfold, playing through once a day. The room architecture places the viewer uncomfortably close to this large image, overwhelming in its scale. The original event becomes monumental, in time as well as space.

An architectural structure enclosing time, *Passage* is a hybrid between the forms of installation and single-channel videotape. The installation is constructed in the physical form of an archetypal emblem of transition and transformation, the tunnel or long narrow passageway, which ultimately refers to the original passage through the birth canal. The structure frames an image that transcends human scale in both time and space, placing it in the internal or subjective domain of memory and emotive association. The child's birthday party, a familiar rite of passage and a contemporary vestige of an ancient perennial ritual, regains some of its ritualistic and mythic stature through the manipulation of space and the extreme extension of time.

41 The Sleep of Reason

1988
Video/sound installation

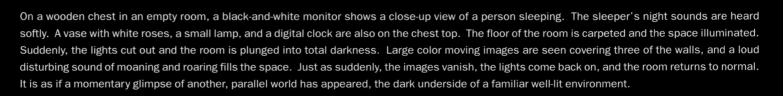

On a wooden chest in an empty room, a black-and-white monitor shows a close-up view of a person sleeping. The sleeper's night sounds are heard softly. A vase with white roses, a small lamp, and a digital clock are also on the chest top. The floor of the room is carpeted and the space illuminated. Suddenly, the lights cut out and the room is plunged into total darkness. Large color moving images are seen covering three of the walls, and a loud disturbing sound of moaning and roaring fills the space. Just as suddenly, the images vanish, the lights come back on, and the room returns to normal. It is as if a momentary glimpse of another, parallel world has appeared, the dark underside of a familiar well-lit environment.

The blackouts occur at random periods, behaving like unpredictable "image seizures" from some incurable schizophrenic affliction of the room. Present for only a few seconds, they can reoccur anywhere from less than one second to several minutes later, impossible to anticipate. The three projections of imagery on the walls are from a single videotape. Images include fires burning out of control through city buildings, fierce attack dogs lunging at the camera, wild movement through a forest at night, moving X-rays of human beings and animals, and a provoked owl flying into a bright light.

structure of heaven, earth, and hell. The left panel focuses on light and nature and depicts early morning in a small town at the foothills of the mountains. A tranquil landscape of trees, hills, and a few houses is visible, as cars on a freeway constantly move through the landscape like an artificial river. The image on the right panel shows the nocturnal forces of destruction—a blazing fire on a city street at night. Flames are seen on the roofs of buildings and the sky glows orange. Man-made structures collapse as firefighters battle the blaze with their equipment. Positioned between these two extremes are the affairs of men here on earth, represented on the central panel as a meeting of a political council in the formal setting of a large municipal hall, where budgets are voted on and formal presentations are discussed. The three video sequences are synchronized together and play back in an endless loop.

43   Angel's Gate

1989

Videotape

A succession of individual images focusing on mortality, decay, and disintegration is delineated by long, slow fades to black. The image sequences—fruit falling from a tree, a candle being extinguished, a family having a flash photograph taken—appear as a series of openings or momentary glimpses into nature's essential gestures which, like thoughts, are destined to fade and disintegrate into obscurity and oblivion. Peak moments illuminate the dim confines of memory and forgetting as a baby emerges into the world before our eyes and the camera eye moves along a dark concrete tunnel toward the rigid steel bars of a locked gate, where it effortlessly passes through and out into the bright world, liberated by the consuming, saturated white light of its own overexposure.

44

Sanctuary

1989

Video/sound installation

A small forest of living pine trees is placed indoors in a large industrial space, sustained by an irrigation system and illuminated by natural light from overhead skylights. Filters placed over the skylights create the hues of early dawn, effusing the space with soft blue light. Viewers enter off the street and are confronted with the sight and smell of full-size trees growing indoors in a mound of earth. Sound and activity can be heard at the rear of the space. There, placed within the trees and partially concealed by them, is a small video projection screen showing a videotape of a woman in labor preparing to give birth. Her sounds, at times quiet, at times violent, are heard through the trees and out over the space and distant city sounds. After a long time, the baby arrives in a culminating moment of peak intensity, and a few minutes later new eyes first open to the outside light.

The video images repeat throughout the day and the trees continue to grow during the course of the installation. The installation is an attempt to create a space in the urban industrialized world where the act of childbirth can be seen as an integral part of nature, participating in the larger cycles of fertility, creation, and growth common to all living things.

45 The Stopping Mind

1991
Video/sound installation

The Stopping Mind is a video installation for projected images and sound based on the age-old human desire to stop time. It deals with the paradox of thought (memory) and experience—the underlying propensity of the mind to retain or arrest experience in the face of the dynamic nature of both the experience and the perpetual movement of consciousness itself.

Four large screens are suspended from the ceiling, parallel to the four walls of the room. They are positioned to describe the sides of a cube open at the corners. Four separate but related images are displayed on the screens. The images are static and the room is silent, except for the sound of a voice quietly whispering in a rapid, unceasing chant that describes the passive loss of bodily sensation in an unknown black space. Suddenly, without warning, the images simultaneously lunge into movement, momentarily coming to life in a wild burst of frantic motion and loud cascading sound. After only a few seconds, and equally without warning, they freeze again and become silent and still as fixed frames. The image sequences are all shot with a constantly moving camera. They are characterized by incessant activity and violent motion, and center on the theme of physical struggle with the material world. They often include oblique images of an individual engaged in such a struggle.

The imprisoned time of the still images can unleash itself at any moment and, once witnessed, the potential for the resumption of their violent activity is imminent and constantly present in the space. The intervals between each onslaught of motion are random and unpredictable, occurring anywhere from several seconds to over a minute apart. If allowed to play continuously, the material would be overwhelming and unbearable. The constant soft monotone of the chanting voice is focused acoustically in the center of the room and provides the only stable reference point in the space.

46 The Passing

1991
Videotape

In memory of Wynne Lee Viola

A personal response to the spiritual extremes of birth and death in the family. Black-and-white nocturnal imagery and underwater scenes depict a twilight world hovering on the borders of human perception and consciousness, where the multiple lives of the mind (memory, reality, and vision) merge.

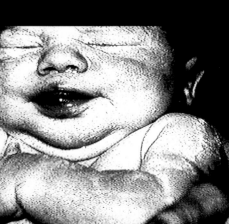

47

Heaven and Earth

1992

Video installation

A columnlike structure is enclosed in a small alcove. It is made of wood and extends from floor to ceiling. There is a gap of several inches at eye level in the column, dividing the structure in two. At this gap, positioned facing each other and not touching, are the exposed tubes of two black-and-white video monitors. The upper monitor shows a close-up image of an old woman on the verge of death, and the lower monitor shows a close-up image of a new baby only days old. The images are silent. Since the surface of each monitor screen is glass, a reflected image of the screen opposite to it can be seen through the surface of each image, as life and death reflect and contain each other.

48

What Is Not and That Which Is

1992

Video/sound installation

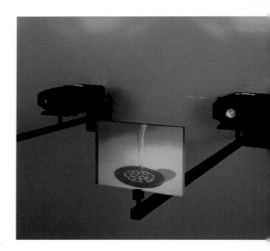

In a darkened room, seven steel armatures extend in a row from the wall and support seven small screens (2 ³/₄ x 5 inches) and their projectors. Each screen shows a different image sequence, a detailed miniature "image world," mostly viewed from a fixed, tableau-style viewpoint. Sound can be heard from tiny speakers at each projector. The seven images, all containing aspects of the passage of time and the destructive forces of nature, particularly water, are referenced through a central image of a man seated at a table alone at night quietly eating a meal.

The individual image sequences are of a series of glass containers falling and shattering on the floor in slow motion; a naked man floating lifelessly underwater; a vortex of water spiraling down a drain; the man eating alone at a table; waves crashing at the shore of a stormy sea; a man struggling in violently rushing water; and a massive rock passing through the alternations of day and night. The images together form a self-portrait, with each image corresponding to an inner state of being that coexists as complementary and conflicting parts of a self endowed with the liberating insights of conscious awareness, yet subject to the corrosive and degenerative forces of the material world.

An electronic display sign mounted across a wall scrolls news information with up-to-date reports on the daily events of the world. The text on the illuminated sign is harsh and bright. A black open doorway intersects the sign, divides it in two, and leads to a dark inner room, forcing the viewer to pass through the gap in the scrolling news reports. Inside this room, gradually visible in the darkness, are three large, dim black-and-white projections of sleeping figures on the interior walls. The sound of regular breathing can be heard in the darkness, defining the room as an internal space, a gallery of unconscious presences existing beneath the incessant flow of worldly events.

50

To Pray Without Ceasing

1992

Video/sound installation

A contemporary "book of hours" and image vigil to the infinite day, functioning as an unfolding sequence of prayers for the city. A twelve-hour cycle of images plays twice daily, projected onto a screen mounted to a window facing the street. The images are projected continuously, twenty-four hours a day, seven days a week. A voice can be heard quietly reciting a text (excerpts from Walt Whitman's "Song of Myself"), audible from speakers mounted above on each side of the window, interior and exterior.

During the day, sunlight washes out the image and only the voice is present. At dusk, the images gradually become visible as the light fades, reaching peak intensity and contrast after dark. The video playback is synchronized to the time of day by computer. All images are locked to clock time and repeat at exactly the same time each day. Geographic location and the season when the work is installed determine the amount of the image sequences visible and/or obscured by the sunlight. The voice is heard continuously.

There are twelve sections or "prayers" in the work. They vary in length from fifteen minutes to two hours and describe a cycle of individual and universal life, beginning in light and fire and culminating in darkness and water. The sections are: Light/Fire; Land/Nature; Animals; Birth; Childhood; Communities; Travel/Passage; Individual Self; Physical Body; Decay/Disintegration; Dissolution/Submergence; and Water/Darkness.

51

Nantes Triptych

1992

Video/sound installation

Three large-scale panels of projected video images form a configuration based on the triptych altarpiece form. The left panel shows an image of a young woman in the process of giving birth. The right panel shows an image of an old woman in the process of dying. Both are documents of actual events.

On the central panel, an image of a clothed man underwater is seen moving through alternate stages of turbulence and undulating stillness. The figure is suspended in a void, illuminated in stark light. This panel is made of a translucent cloth scrim material, allowing much of the image's light to pass through into a separate inaccessible space, forming an indistinct luminous cloud just visible behind and through this screen surface. The projected image of the body underwater hovers in midair, part material, part immaterial, held in fragile suspension before an indistinct, shadowy space, suspended between birth and death.

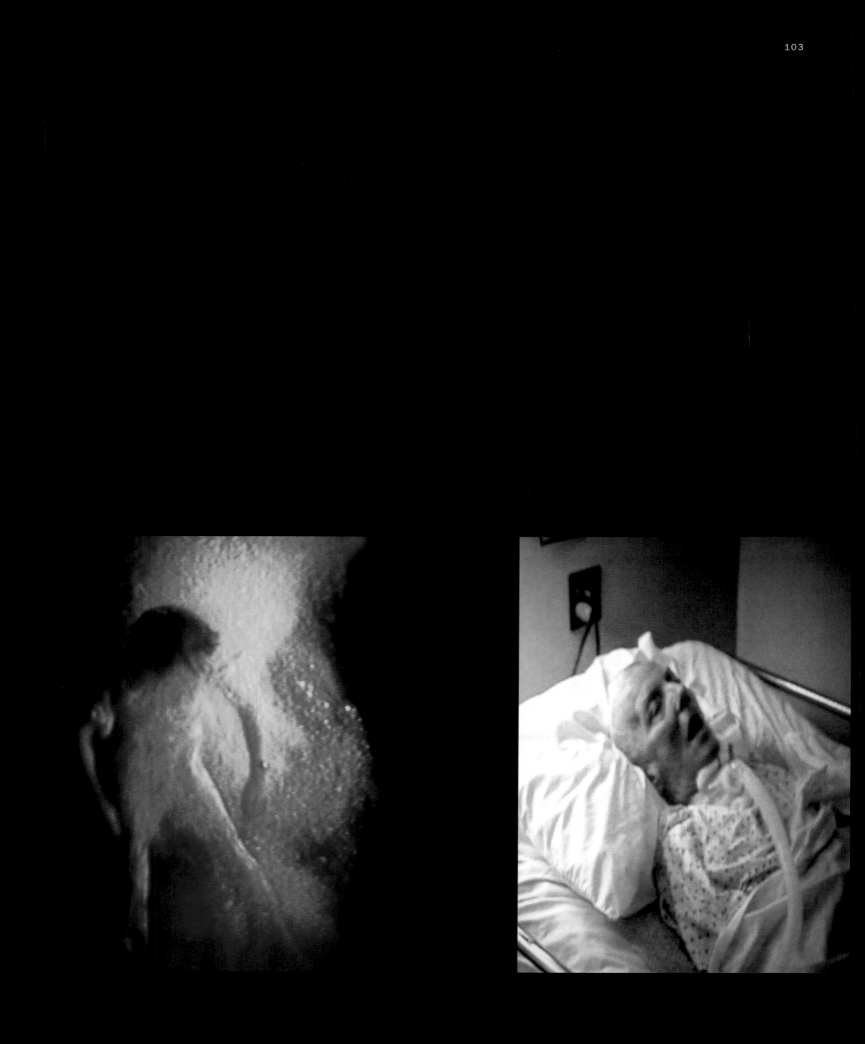

52

The Sleepers

1992
Video installation

Seven 55-gallon metal barrels stand in a darkened room. They are white inside and out and are open at the top. The only light in the space is a soft bluish glow emerging from each barrel and diffused throughout the room. The barrels are filled to the brim with water. Under the water at the bottom of each one is a black-and-white video monitor facing straight up, the source of the blue light. Video and power cables for the monitor are visible as they emerge from the floor and enter the water over the top rim of each barrel. Each submerged monitor screen shows a close-up of a person's face as they sleep. There is an image of a different person in each barrel, actual recordings of people sleeping presented continuously with little or no editing. Occasionally, the sleepers move or shift position, but they remain asleep, isolated from each other on their individual screens beneath the water.

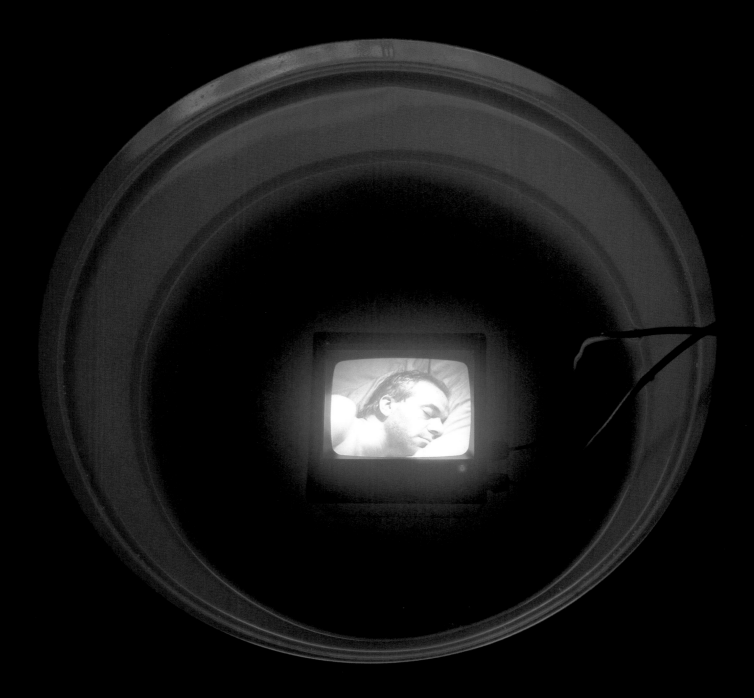

The Arc of Ascent

1992

Video/sound installation

Two complementary moving-image sequences involving the human figure are seen in monumental scale (9 feet wide by 22½ feet high) on a projection screen in a dark room. First, the image of a man is seen upside down, floating serenely in free fall in extreme slow motion, suspended against a void, subtly moving on a passage through an eternal moment. Suddenly, he crashes through the surface of the water and submerges into a darkened pool, the image and sound exploding in a piercing white splash and roaring turbulent aftermath. The figure is projected as an inverted image, so that descent becomes ascent and the man's body moves upward toward a violent conclusion, in which he appears to pass up and out of the room, breaking an unseen barrier between two worlds.

The second image also shows a clothed man, this time floating underwater in a dark pool. The image is inverted so that the water surface is visible at the bottom of the picture. He slowly shifts and turns, submerged in a dark void, making no movements other than allowing the water currents to move his body. Gradually, his form turns more forcefully as white turbulence begins appearing around him, and he is suddenly and swiftly drawn down in a swirling white cloud of bubbles and roaring turbulence. Here, the image is not only inverted but time is run backwards, so that he is seen to plunge into the water in reverse, his body being rapidly sucked out through the surface, leaving not a ripple. In this way, he appears to pass down through the floor and out of the room, again breaking an unseen barrier between the worlds.

54 Slowly Turning Narrative

1992
Video/sound installation

A large screen (9 x 12 feet wide) is slowly rotating on a central axis in the center of a large dark room. Two video projectors are facing it from opposite sides of the space. One side of the screen is a mirrored surface, the other side a normal projection screen. One projector shows a constant black-and-white image of a man's face in close-up, in harsh light, appearing distracted and at times straining. The other projector shows a series of changing color images (young children moving by on a carousel, a house on fire, people at a carnival at night, kids playing with fireworks, etc.), characterized by continuous motion and swirling light and color. On the black-and-white side, a voice can be heard reciting a rhythmic repetitive chant of a long list of phrases descriptive of states of being and individual actions. On the color-image side, the ambient sounds associated with each image are heard.

The beams from the two projectors distort and spill out images across the shifting screen surface and onto the walls as the angle of the screen alternately widens and narrows during the course of its rotations. The mirrored side sends distorted reflections continually cascading across the surrounding walls—indistinct gossamer forms that travel around the perimeter of the room. In addition, viewers in the space see themselves and the space around them reflected in the mirror as it slowly moves past.

The work is concerned with the enclosing nature of self-image and the external circulation of potentially infinite (and therefore unattainable) states of being, all revolving around the still point of the central self. The room and all persons within it become a continually shifting projection screen, enclosing the image and its reflections, all locked into the regular cadence of the chanting voice and the rotating screen. The entire space becomes an interior for the revelations of a constantly turning mind absorbed with itself. The confluences and conflicts of image, intent, content, and emotion perpetually circulate as the screen slowly turns in the space.

55 Tiny Deaths

1993
Video/sound installation

Three large projections appear on the walls of a dark room, each showing images of the human figure as it is suddenly exposed to a burst of high-intensity light. The normal state of the room is absolute darkness. The projections exist at the threshold of perception, barely visible at first and becoming clearer the longer one stays in the room. Human forms are seen to gradually emerge from blackness as dim silhouettes on a field of noise.

At random intervals, a light source slowly appears on the body of one of the figures, increasing until the illumination rapidly expands and accelerates to suddenly consume the whole body in a burst of saturated, blinding white light. The peak light momentarily illuminates the room and washes out the other two projections. All returns abruptly to darkness until another projected image moves through the same transformation. Quiet, indecipherable voices are heard by each image, as if someone were talking in another room. The voices build in volume yet remain unclear, culminating in a final burst of sound that punctuates the flash of white light and is followed instantaneously by the return to silence and darkness.

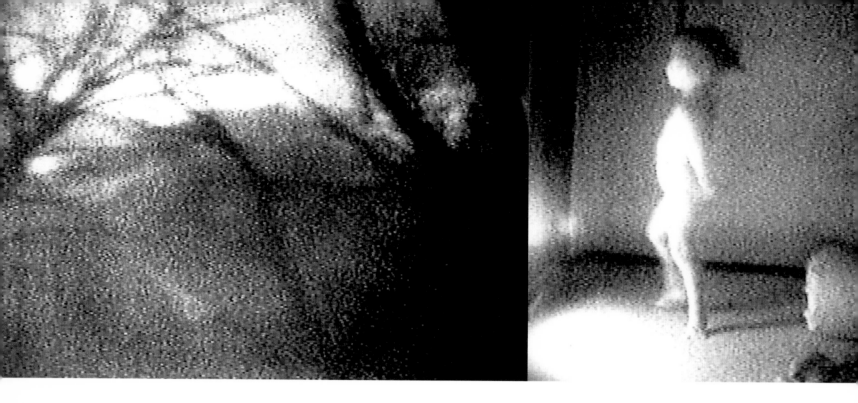

Pneuma

1994

Video/sound installation

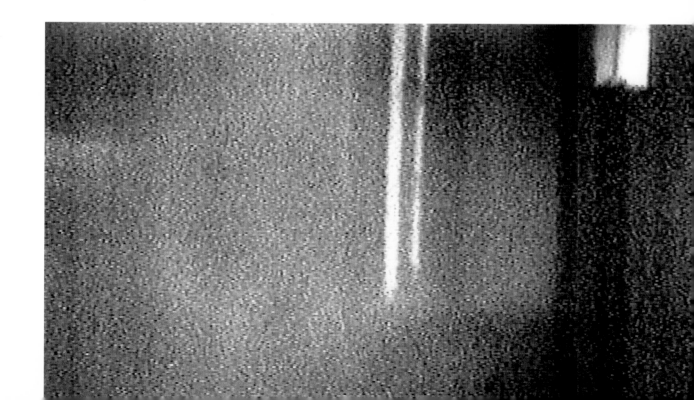

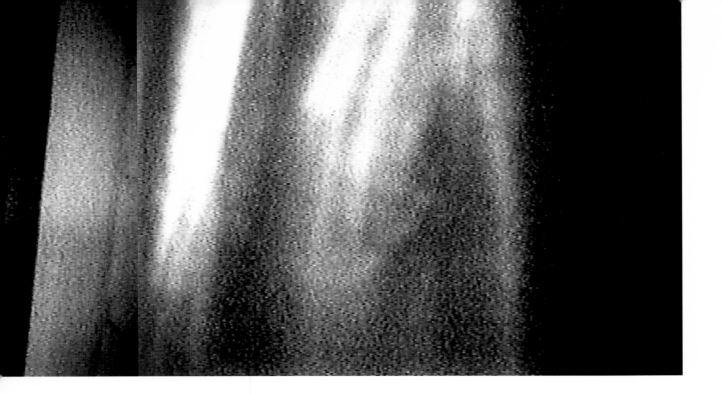

Moving images are projected in monochrome into the three corners of a dark room. Viewers enter through a door at the fourth corner. The projections fill the walls and overlap with each other, creating a continuous image field that wraps around the room, ending at the entrance area. The sound of white noise permeates the space, and the images appear to coalesce out of a vibrating cloud of abstract grain. Images such as children playing, distant buildings, reflections in a water fountain, and a field of flowers remain fleeting and ambiguous, like a dim memory or a forgotten dream.

"Pneuma" is an ancient Greek word that has no equivalent in contemporary terms. Commonly translated as soul or spirit, it refers as well to breath, and was conceived as an underlying essence or life force which runs through all things of nature, animating or illuminating them with Mind. In the installation, images alternately emerge and submerge into a field of shimmering visual noise, the ground of all images, and hover at the threshold of recognition and ambiguity. Indistinct, shifting, and shadowy, the projections become more like memories or internal sensations rather than recorded images of actual places and events, surrounding and submerging the viewer in their essence.

57   # Stations

1994

Video/sound installation

Stations is an installation for five channels of video projection and sound, focusing on images of the human body submerged underwater. Five cloth screens are suspended from the ceiling of a large, dark, open space. Under each, a slab of polished black granite lies flat on the floor. The granite slabs are the same dimensions as the screens, on which five different images of the human figure underwater can be seen. The figures are lit with a strong cross light and stand out against the dark void of the background. The submerged bodies hang limp, suspended in space in the subjective tense of slow motion. They are projected upside down and their righted reflections can simultaneously be seen on the polished stone surface below. Underwater sounds are heard locally near each screen.

The images play continuously, and at varying intervals the bodies are seen to slowly drift out of the frame, eventually leaving the room dark and silent. Suddenly, the figures plunge into the water in an explosion of light and turbulence. Gradually, the disturbance subsides as they are again slowly at drift until the cycle repeats itself. There is no single viewing angle to the piece, and viewers are free to enter and move about the space at will. An initial surface appearance of eerie, serene beauty resides over a deeper disturbing aspect of muted violence and disorder, with the unrooted, isolated, free-floating bodies evoking an eternal state between dream and death.

Déserts

1994

Concert film/videotape

Music by Edgard Varèse

but was unable to realize the visual component in his lifetime. He left only very general references to the images he envisioned for the music, preferring to leave the specifics to the filmmaker, as in the following statement:

"For me, deserts is a highly evocative word. It suggests space, solitude, detachment. To me it means not only deserts of sand, sea, mountains
and snow, of outer space, of deserted city streets, not only those stripped aspects of nature that suggest bareness and aloofness but also the
remote inner space of the mind no telescope can reach, a world of mystery and essential loneliness."

Premiered in 1954, Varèse's *Déserts* is notable for its use of taped sound collages that interrupt the live music at three points in the score. The
film uses this basic structure to describe the stark contrast between the interior space of a man alone in a windowless room, and diverse scenes of
an expansive external world devoid of people—shimmering desert vistas, undulating underwater landscapes, stark vacant streets at night, and the
intense luminous heat of a raging fire. Here, images of desolation and violent destruction do not necessarily signify either negation, loss, or final
annihilation, but rather they become vehicles of transcendence and transformation, ultimately focused on a deepening knowledge of the self. In the
end, the stark relief established between interior and exterior, solitude and space, breaks down in a crescendo of destruction and liberation, both
musically and visually, as surface appearances are shattered and the two isolated worlds of above and below the water merge into one.

59 Hall of Whispers

1995

Video/sound installation

Viewers enter a long, narrow dark room, and must pass between ten video projections arranged in two rows along the side walls, five on either side of the room. The projections are life-size black-and-white images of people's heads facing the viewer, with their eyes closed and their mouths tightly bound and gagged. They are straining to speak, but their muffled voices are incomprehensible, and mingle in the space in a low, indecipherable jumble of sound.

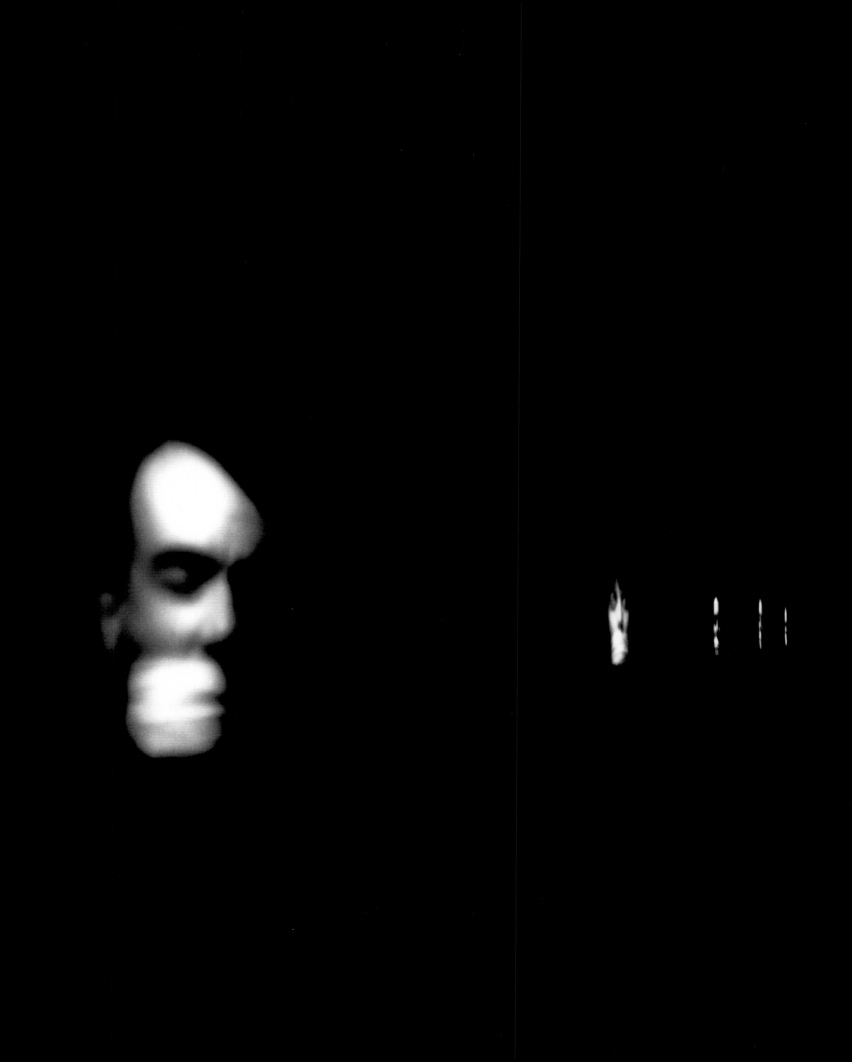

Interval

1995

Video/sound installation

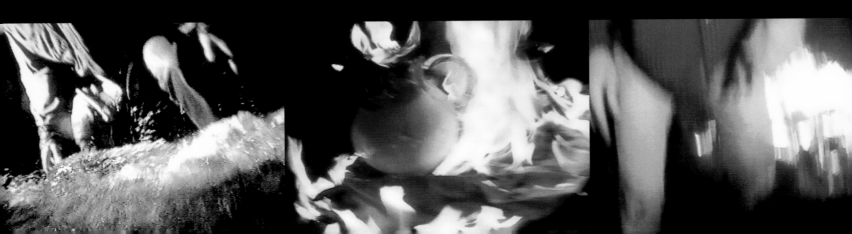

Two large color projections stand opposite each other, filling the side walls of a small room. Viewers pass between the images on their way through the space. An image of a man alone in a shower room, naked, is seen on one wall as he slowly and methodically cleans his body with a white cloth and a bucket of water. A series of wild and violent images appears on the other wall, showing a figure struggling through fire and water intercut with scenes of the camera point of view aggressively pushing itself through folds of skin into the body's orifices.

The two sets of images represent not only opposing architectural surfaces, but embody opposing energies—peaceful/violent, passive/aggressive, calm/chaotic. Controlled by a computer-programmed switcher, the images are never present on opposite walls simultaneously. Instead they appear sequentially, one at a time, displayed according to a mathematically programmed curve that alternates their duration in ever decreasing intervals of time. Starting at one minute, the images and sound switch slowly at first, then faster and faster, finally reaching the limit of the frame rate of the video signal at thirty times per second. This extreme peak condition is maintained for a few moments until both images abruptly end in black and silence and the cycle starts anew.

What begins as a simple, slow succession of images gradually becomes a violent, roaring alternation, eventually reaching a blurred merger of the two as the peak switching frequency is reached, exceeding the ability of the human eye and ear to distinguish between distinct pictures and sounds, and creating the impression that the two images are, for a brief moment, coexisting simultaneously.

61   The Veiling

1995
Video/sound installation

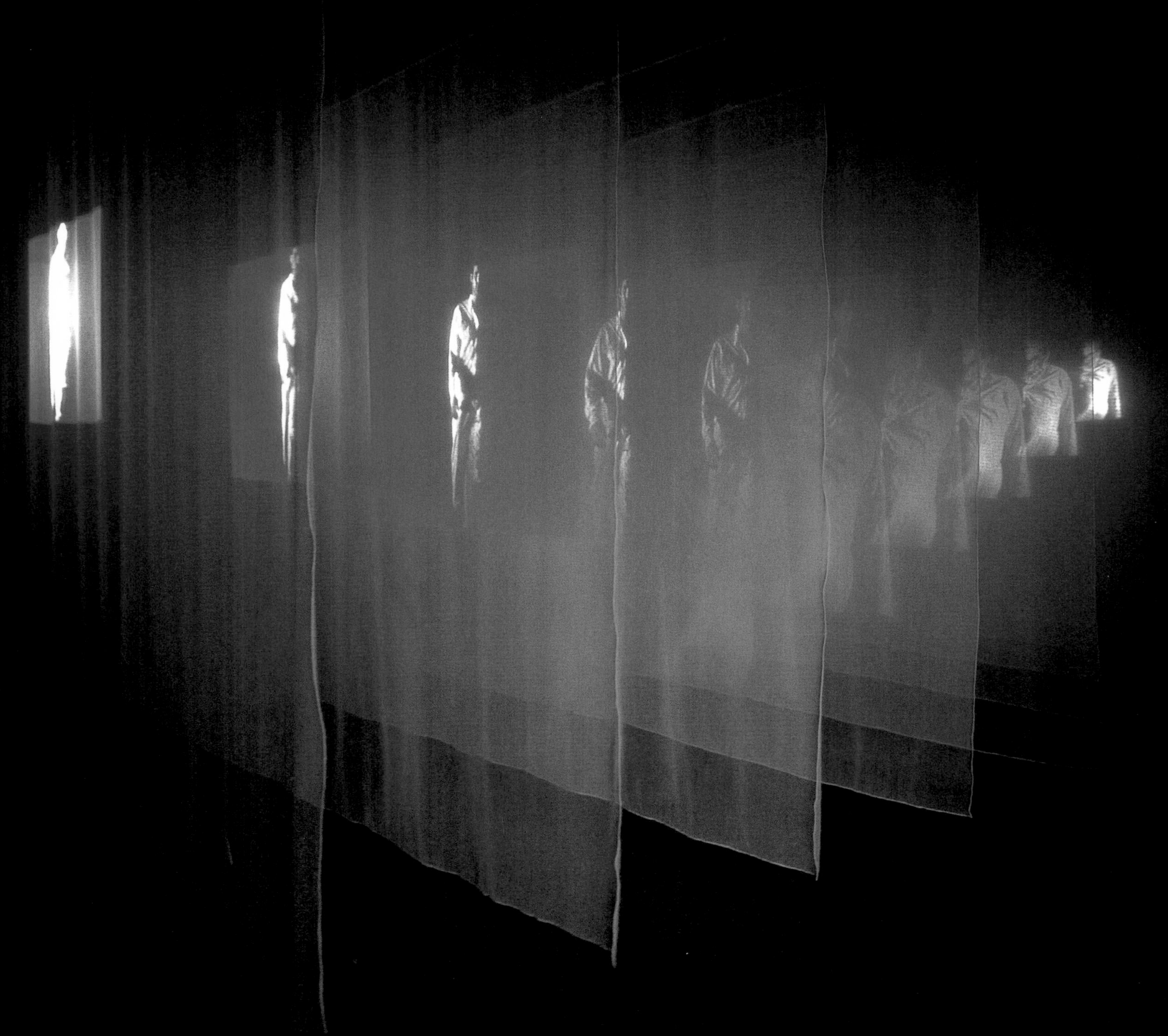

The Veiling

Thin parallel layers of translucent cloth hang loosely across the center of a dark room. Two projectors at opposite ends of the space face each other and project images into the layers of material. The images show a man and a woman as they approach and move away from the camera, viewed in various nocturnal landscapes. They each appear on separate opposing video channels, and are seen gradually moving from dark areas of shadow into areas of bright light. The cloth material diffuses the light, and the images dissipate in intensity and focus as they penetrate further into the scrim layers, eventually intersecting each other as gossamer presences on the central veil. Recorded independently, the images of the man and the woman never coexist in the same video frame. It is only the light from their images that intermingles in the fabric of the hanging veils. The cone of light emerging from each projector is articulated in space by the layers of material, revealing its presence as a three-dimensional form that moves through and fills the empty space of the room with its translucent mass.

62   # The Greeting

1995

Video/sound installation

Inspired by Pontormo's Mannerist painting *Visitation* (1528-29), *The Greeting* is a video image sequence projected onto a screen mounted to the wall of a dark room. Two women are seen engaged in conversation. Industrial buildings are visible behind them, aligned in a strange perspective within a barren urban background. As the two women are talking, they are interrupted by a third woman who enters and approaches them. As they prepare to greet her, it becomes apparent that one of the women knows her quite well, the other less so or perhaps not at all. A slight wind comes up and the light subtly shifts as the new woman arrives to greet the one she knows, ignoring the other. As the two embrace, she leans and whispers something to her friend, further isolating the other woman. With an underlying awkwardness, introductions are then made and pleasantries exchanged among the three.

Presented as a single take from a fixed camera position and projected in a vertical aspect ratio more common to painting, the actions of the figures are seen in extreme slow motion. An original event of forty-five seconds now unfolds as an elaborate choreography over the course of ten minutes. Subtle aspects of the scene become apparent. The unconscious body language and nuances of fleeting glances and gestures become heightened and remain suspended in the viewer's conscious awareness. Minor shifts in light and wind conditions become central events. At times the background becomes foreground, and other figures are seen in the darker spaces behind the central figures, engaged in unknown activities. The geometry of the walls and buildings appears to violate the laws of optical perspective, and this, together with ambiguities in lighting, all lend a subjective character to the overall scene. In the end, none of the figure's actions or intentions is explained or becomes apparent. The precise meaning of the event remains in circulation as an ambiguous, speculative gesture.

63 # The Messenger

1996
Video/sound installation

The Messenger was originally created for Durham Cathedral, in northern England. A large image was projected onto a screen mounted to the great west door of the church. The image sequence begins with a small, luminous, abstract form shimmering and undulating against a deep blue-black void. Gradually, the luminous shape begins to get larger and less distorted, and it soon becomes apparent that we are seeing a human form, illuminated, rising toward us from under the surface of a body of water. The water becomes calmer and more transparent and the figure clearer on its journey upwards toward us. We identify the figure as a man, pale blue, naked, on his back, rising up slowly.

After some time, he breaks the surface, an act at once startling, relieving, and desperate. His pale form emerges into the warm hues of a bright light, the water glistening on his body. His eyes immediately open as he releases a long-held breath from the depths, shattering the silence of the image. The forceful primal sound of life resonates momentarily in the space. After a few moments, he inhales deeply, and, with his eyes shut and mouth closed, he sinks into the depths of the blue-black void once more, returning to his origin as a shimmering, moving point of light. The image sequence continually repeats, with the man perpetually rising and sinking, describing the constant circulation of birth and death, and functioning like a great cycle of respiration in the space.

64

The Crossing

1996

Video/sound installation

A large double-sided projection screen stands in the middle of the room, its bottom edge resting on the floor. Two video projectors mounted at opposite ends of the room project images onto the front and back sides of the screen simultaneously, showing a single action involving a human figure culminating in a violent annihilation by the opposing natural forces of fire and water.

On one side of the screen, a human form slowly approaches from a great distance through a dark space. The figure gradually becomes more distinct, and we soon recognize a man walking straight toward us, all the time becoming larger. When his body almost fills the frame, he stops moving and stands still, staring directly at the viewer in silence. A small votive flame appears at his feet. Suddenly, brilliant orange flames rise up and quickly spread across the floor and up onto his body. A loud roaring sound fills the space as his form rapidly becomes completely engulfed by a violent raging fire. The fire soon subsides until only a few small flickering flames remain on a charred floor. The figure of the man is gone. The image returns to black and the cycle repeats anew.

On the other side, we again see a dark human form approaching. He slowly moves toward us out of the shadows, in the same manner as the other figure. Finally, he too stops and stares, motionless and silent. Suddenly, a stream of silver-blue water begins pouring onto his head, sending luminous trails of splashing droplets off in all directions. The stream quickly turns into a raging torrent as a massive amount of water cascades from above, completely inundating the man as a loud roaring sound fills the space. The falling water soon begins to subside and it trails off, leaving a few droplets falling on a wet floor. The figure of the man is gone. The image then returns to black and the cycle repeats anew.

The two complementary actions appear simultaneously on the two sides of the screen, and the viewer must move around the space to see both images. The image sequences are timed to play in perfect synchronization, with the approach and the culminating conflagration and deluge occurring simultaneously, energizing the space with a violent raging crescendo of intense images and roaring sound. The two traditional natural elements of fire and water appear here not only in their destructive aspects, but manifest their cathartic, purifying, transformative, and regenerative capacities as well. In this way, self-annihilation becomes a necessary means to transcendence and liberation.

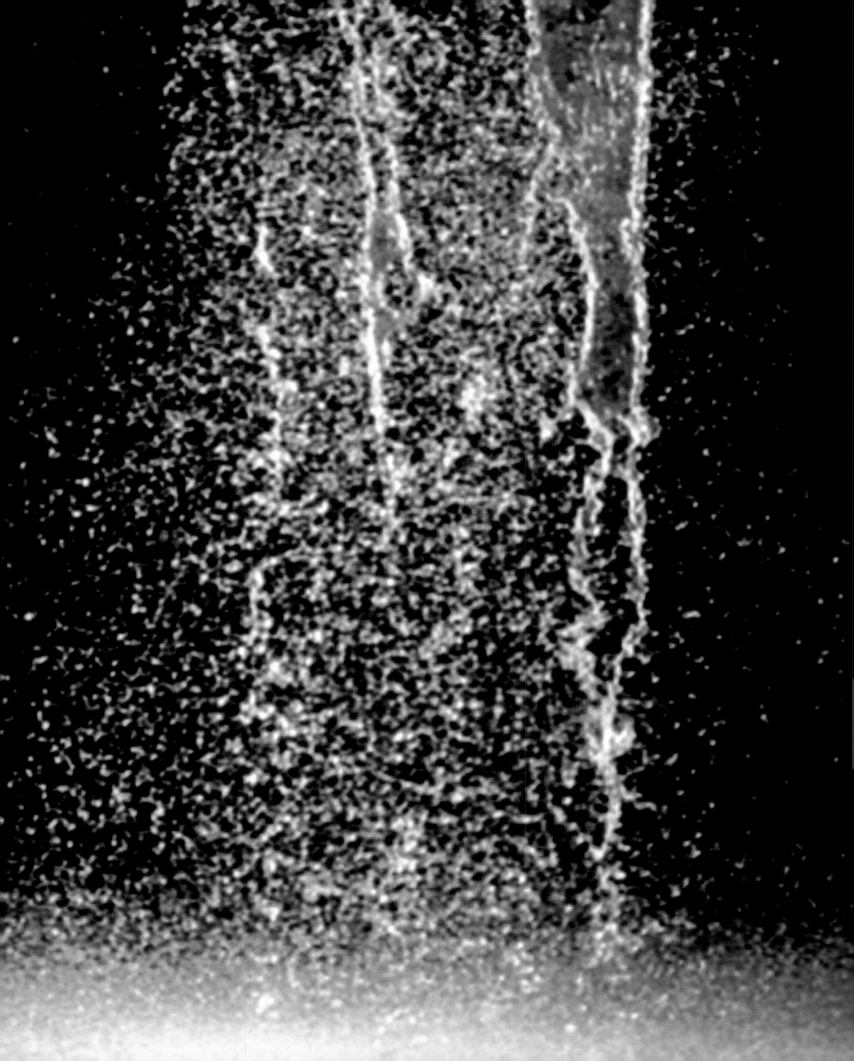

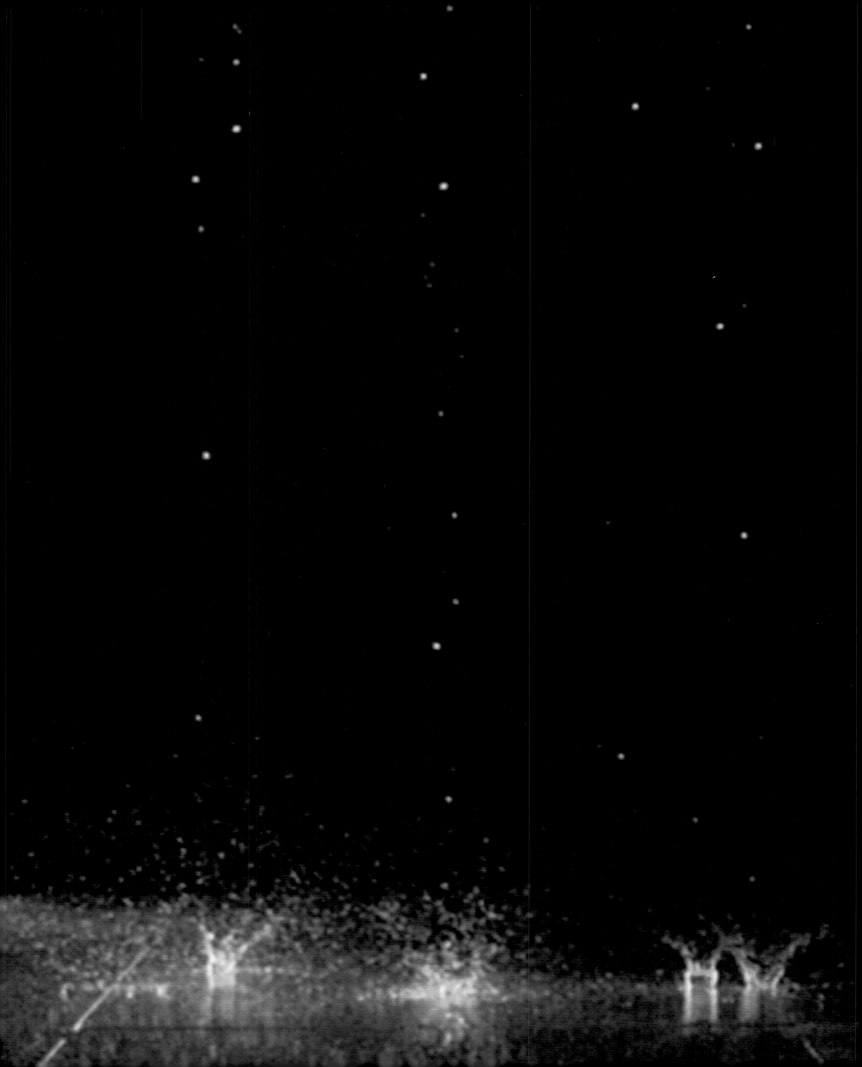

Conversation

Lewis Hyde and Bill Viola

This conversation took place on two occasions in Santa Monica and Long Beach, California, in March 1997. Lewis Hyde had just finished his new book, *Trickster Makes This World: Mischief, Myth, and Art.*

Part 1   March 5, 1997

Lewis Hyde: I want to talk first about the connections in your work to spiritual life. From an earlier piece like *Room for St. John of the Cross* to a recent one like *The Messenger*, which was made for Durham Cathedral in England, there seems to be a religious side to your artistic practice. Can you talk a bit about what spiritual traditions matter to you?

Bill Viola: Well, first off, I never felt a formal adherence to any particular tradition. I was raised Episcopalian because my mother was raised Episcopalian growing up in England, but I never really had a functional relationship to religion while growing up, as with many in my generation. My mother did instill in me a deep spiritual sense of the world, beyond the specifics of her religion. She was and is very special to me in this way. But it wasn't until university that I started to encounter Eastern religions. This was the late sixties, and this stuff was just floating around in the air. The two big currents I remember at the time were the Indian connection through the Upanishads, the Bhagavad Gita, and Ravi Shankar's music, and the Japanese Zen connection through the writings of D.T. Suzuki and the Beats and John Cage.

Personally, I remember several things: Kenzo Tange's books on Japanese Buddhist gardens; the Dover edition of E.H. Whinfield's nineteenth-century translation of Rumi's *Masnavi*; the Nonesuch World Explorer records of Asian music, particularly Balinese and Javanese gamelan music; the Penguin Books paperback edition of Lao Tzu's *Tao Te Ching*, which I carried everywhere; the Jung/Wilhelm *I Ching*; and P.D. Ouspensky's *A New Model of the Universe*, a kind of compendium of Eastern philosophy and esoteric traditions written in 1931 that included Einsteinian "new" physics. It was subtitled *Principles of the Psychological Method in Its Application to Problems of Science, Religion and Art.*

As a child I had always been in my own world, preferring to stay at home and draw rather than play. I loved being alone in empty spaces. And I guess what happened to me when I encountered these formal ancient systems was like a shock of recognition. I couldn't believe that somebody had actually worked out a system for dealing with what we call subjective experience, and sometimes in very complex and technically precise ways, as in Tibetan Buddhism. It was new and different but somehow deeply familiar, and it verified certain feelings I had as a kid that used to make me think that I was different and disconnected from the world described by my own culture. The point that is significant here is that culture comes from people and is formed by the individual's engagement with the world—it doesn't come out of some intellectual concept that someone invented out of nowhere. Once I realized that personal experiences and inner feelings can be objectified out in the world, then I wanted to read everything I could get my hands on. I took a workshop in meditation. It was primarily through these studies and readings that I eventually went to Japan and met the Zen master Daien Tanaka and actually started practicing Zen meditation.

I guess the connection ultimately, if I can say it in one encapsulated way, has to do with an acknowledgment or awareness or recognition that there is something above, beyond, below, beneath what's in front of our eyes, what our daily life is focused on. There's another dimension that you just know is there, that can be a source of real knowledge, and the quest for connecting with that and identifying that is the whole impetus for me to cultivate these experiences and to make my work. And, on a larger scale, it is also the driving force behind all religious endeavors. There is an unseen world out there and we are living in it.

You know, in the Middle Ages they painted the sky gold in the paintings. Today our photographs show a blue sky. We think the gold is an abstraction. To the medieval eye, the

blue sky was the abstraction. It was realism they were after—the reality of the divine effused through everything in the physical world. In the Middle Ages, East and West were on common ground, and ironically it was through my encounter with Eastern philosophy, particularly the great Eastern émigrés to the West, D.T. Suzuki and A.K. Coomaraswamy, that I rediscovered the roots of my own Christian tradition. Suzuki and Coomaraswamy, sensing that this other way of being must also be here somewhere, began to research the Western tradition and uncover a forgotten path, and through them I discovered people like the Desert Fathers and the Gnostics of Early Christianity, Meister Eckhart, St. John of the Cross, Saint Teresa, and *The Cloud of Unknowing*, the classic medieval text in the Christian tradition of the *via negativa*.

LH: What is the *via negativa* in the Christian tradition?

BV: The *via negativa* in the West is connected to a shadowy fifth-century character known as Pseudo-Dionysius the Aeropagite, who many believe was a Syrian monk. He gave us the concept of the "celestial hierarchy," defining a system of correspondences, in a series of levels or stages, between the individual and God. He described an immanent God, the deity that is within each person (an Eastern concept), as opposed to the transcendent God of the more familiar *via positiva*, over and above all and outside the individual. The *via positiva* describes God as the ultimate expression of a series of attributes or qualities—good, all-seeing, all-knowing, etc.—of which human beings contain lesser, diminished versions. It is a distinction of quantity, not quality. The *via negativa*, on the other hand, is the way of negation. God is wholly other and cannot be described or comprehended. There are no attributes other than unknowability. When the mind faces the divine reality, it seizes up and enters a "cloud of unknowing," or, to use St. John of the Cross' term, "a dark night of the soul." Here in the darkness, the only thing to go

on is faith, and the only way to approach God is from within, primarily through love. This is why much of St. John's poetry reads like classic love poems.

In this way, through deep practice and effort, and "letting go," the individual can achieve union with God, sometimes described in the metaphor of ecstatic sex. Eastern religions call it enlightenment. You can see how the role of the established institution of the Church and the authority of the priests could be threatened by this, and during the Inquisition practitioners of the *via negativa* were persecuted. St. John of the Cross was imprisoned and tortured for nine months in 1577. The *via positiva* won out and is the model in use for the most part in Christianity today.

LH: What about the Sufis?

BV: Jalaluddin Rumi, the thirteenth-century Persian poet and mystic, is one of my all-time heroes. I started reading him when I was in college, and he remains my supreme source of inspiration and to my mind one of the greatest literary and religious figures of all time. But I didn't discover the larger tradition of Islamic Sufism and the teaching stories until a couple of years after I graduated. I was working in Florence at Art/Tapes/22 video studio in 1975, and this young man came to visit our studio. He stayed about two days. I forget his name but he was a very strange person. He had learned how to make his eyes point in different directions, and in every official photo, passport included, you saw this lazy eye which he never really had. He traveled with flash paper, and at unexpected times he would pull some out and ignite it, causing a huge orange flame to momentarily appear in the air next to him, startling everyone. You would turn to look and it would be gone, and he would act like nothing happened. He had a book of Sufi stories by Idries Shah and gave it to me before he left. The stories were amazing on many levels, true teaching stories—wise, goofy, serious,

funny, inscrutable, like allegories or parables. They were so direct, so simple. The same stories used by the highest masters in the order to teach the deepest knowledge also served to teach small children the basics of the language. Someone else gave me *The Sense of Unity*, a book by N. Ardalan and L. Bakhtiar on Persian Sufi-inspired architecture, and that's where I discovered S.H. Nasr, who wrote the introduction and quoted many more stories and texts, and described the total unified system of philosophy, religion and science that is so distinctive in Islam. I just dove in and followed up every footnote and reference, and I am still doing so to this day. I originally got the book on my way to live in Florence, and my first experiences of the churches and cathedrals there were under its spell. I think that the combination of the cosmological system of Islam and Sufi mysticism it described and the physical experience of those medieval and Renaissance spaces is one of the key source points for my interest in installations. What about yourself?

LH: I encountered the Sufis through friends. My traditions are mostly Zen Buddhism and the Christian mystics, and there was a long time when Meister Eckhart, the fourteenth-century German mystic, was the focus of my reading. I had a book of Eckhart's writings that was published in the 1920s.

BV: By Blakney?

LH: The C. de B. Evans translation. Blakney is later. I used to read Eckhart's sermons and collations during writing retreats, which were self-isolation events in the city—cutting off the telephone and cutting off the newspaper and cutting the connections to the outside world.

BV: Self-initiated?

LH: Yes. To write but also just to read. In Eckhart there were certain models for me. My mind works imagistically, and Eckhart has powerful images of the spiritual world.

But, it's more than models. What I want to talk about is authority. What is it that makes a spiritual work have authority for you? You've already given one answer: you've had this experience growing up and somebody comes along who offers the image, or tells the narrative that not only echoes your own experience but that also deepens it. And similarly with Buddhism. Buddhism for me is a non-theistic practice of being in the world. In my own reading, the Gospels were important for a long time, but I had problems in that I was taking them metaphorically in a way. I didn't connect with the entire structure I was being offered. I have less problem in that line with Buddhism, in that the practice is in accord with my own sense of how the world is. But my question has to do with authority, in particular with the way in which spiritual knowledge or spiritual traditions become present artistically, and what makes spiritual art work or not.

I was going to tell a story. I had a dream once, a disturbing dream which I took to a psychotherapist. I won't go into detail about it here—actually it appears in my *Trickster* book in a little thing called "Interlude." Suffice it to say that the therapist and I worked on an analysis of this dream for some months, chewing over what different things were going on. Somewhere I began to have an intellectual sense of a pattern that made certain connections and I thought we were getting some place. One day, I was telling my wife about the connections I was making to the dream and so forth, and at a certain point in this narrative I began to weep, and I thought, "Well, okay. Now I know I'm in the right area." My image of this "knowing" has something to do with the authority question I'm after. You can do six interpretations of the same dream and how do you know which one is the one that hits the mark?

The material I was working on at the time had to do with Hermes, the Greek god of boundary crossing; one of the things Hermes can do is operate in all three worlds. He can go into the underworld, and he is present on the surface of the earth—of all the Greek deities, the closest to human kind—and he is the messenger of the gods. He moves from heaven to earth to the underworld. He can operate in all these realms, and I linked that image of Hermes being able to connect with three different levels with what had happened with this dream. On the one hand, there was a presenting dream, which was entirely unconscious. It's as if it came from the underworld. Then there's an analysis of it, and that's up in your head. Then there's a moment of weeping, which is entirely in the physical, animal body. Somehow the tears come because the dream and the intellectual reading of it are sufficiently congruent to give you the emotional response. This is why somehow I felt that my reading of this dream was the true reading.

This is a little example. So, the problem with authority is: how does one know when these links are genuine? The short story writer Grace Paley says, "You can never know if it's any good. You can only know if it's true." So you are at home writing your short story and you have no idea whether somebody will like it or not. But on some interior terms you have a sense of your own standards and you work until you fulfill them.

To come back to your work, I recently saw your piece *Room for St. John of the Cross* in a group show called "Negotiating Rapture." Some of the works seemed to me authentically representative of the stated theme, others perhaps not. But as you come into the museum the assertion is being made that each of these pieces is about a spiritual event called "rapture." I began to think that you could take a gum wrapper from the street and say it represents the experience of rapture, which it could in certain circumstances.

So I'm trying to address this issue of how, in a secular age, one works in a spiritual vein, and how one avoids the problem of simply labeling things in a way that tells the audience how to respond. In your own story, you have experiences as a child which on some level remained unnamed and then suddenly something happens which names them and the connection is made. The naming doesn't come first. In fact, maybe for a lot of us, spiritual life doesn't work to the degree that it's an imposed narrative, so if our parents take us to Sunday school it's the experience of obligation, not the experience of spiritual life.

BV: Exactly. And you could touch the spiritual life on your own walking down the street somewhere and your parents would never understand it.

LH: So some place in here is this question I think that has to do with—I keep coming back to this word "authority," and I don't know if that's the right word.

BV: Verification or authenticity?

LH: In that area.

BV: Well, I believe that the feelings I had when I was a child are authentic and universal; that is, they are not just about my own particular feelings of that time and place. Carl Jung might call them archetypes, but in any case they are out there in the world. Many other people have had these feelings before. Sometimes that's resulted in organized institutions, monasteries, religious orders, or religious visions which become institutions, but the point is that, as Mircea Eliade said, "the sacred is a part of the structure of consciousness and not a stage in the evolution of consciousness." In other words, there wasn't a time when things were any more spiritual than they are now. There wasn't a time when there were all these gods around us in this spiritual

world and now consciousness has evolved so we don't need that any more. It's always there. We happen to live in an age that doesn't reflect it or encourage it or focus it in the way that cultures have done in the past where religion has been dominant. But that doesn't mean that it's not there.

I remember being in Ladakh in the Himalayas in 1982 with my wife, Kira. We were taken inside an inner room in a very sacred Tibetan Buddhist monastery. It was a very special occasion, and they were showing us around and there was a series of masks which they used in the dances during the most important religious rituals. A couple of the masks had white cloths over them. We figured that those were the most powerful ones. You could sense it. The monk escorting us got real solemn and very quiet. And something just flashed in my mind at the moment: "What if I just took this white cloth off?" Of course I would never do that, but I imagined what might happen, that it could be a very serious situation and this man could be physically affected in some danger-ous way. I've read about plenty of instances where material objects can literally kill a person if they are charged with some kind of power in the context of a belief system—whereas I felt intuitively that Kira and I standing there would not have perished at that moment. Later I thought about people jumping out of windows to their death when the stock market crashed in 1929, a purely conceptual crisis.

In this sense, what I'm saying is that institutions have built up a system to commandeer these innate feelings we all have and channel them into a certain series of particular experiential forms, objects, iconography, metaphors or structures that become in some ways substitutes for the experiences themselves. If you are not careful this can become idol worship. The Buddha called his teachings a "raft" or "boat"—simply a means to get to the other side. As he said, from then on only a fool would keep carrying the boat around. Statues and images of the Buddha were orig-

inally never considered sacred. They were just physical objects, aids to meditation—the means toward an end. It was only when the religion began to be popularized and reach the masses that they started to be regarded as sacred objects to be worshiped. To the outsider arriving into the local belief system, this all always seems arbitrary and empty, and today in America we are all outsiders, left solely with our intellects as the only way to penetrate beneath the surface.

So I think today that the authority question gets mixed up with belief systems, compounded by this tremendous fluidi-ty and "freedom" we have in the information age. I wonder if something could have spiritual power in the absence of some institutional criterion that everybody can agree on. I remember reading about Greek sculpture and how when the artist completes a statue of Zeus or one of the gods you don't need art critics to tell you if it's good or not because it either has Zeus' energy or it doesn't. Everyone can feel this. That's the first time I could conceive of a world with-out art critics! (Laughs) Seriously, the question of quality or authenticity in art-making in traditional religious contexts usually has more to do with the devotion and practice of the artist than the visual appearance of the end result.

Stephen Mitchell, the contemporary translator, took on the task of uncovering Jesus' authentic words in the Gospels, and he lists his twelve years of meditation with his Zen master as one of his qualifications for undertaking the work. Now that's not a generally acceptable criterion in today's world of scholarship, but if you go to the East, they are saying essentially the same thing—that these words in my book are true because I have had this experience on the spiritual plane which verifies it and therefore I know them to be true. They are looking through one lens, while we are operating in a system that needs a totally different lens to determine authenticity and truth.

Then there's the issue of time and memory and how ideas can reemerge and recirculate, defying linear historical time and achieving a kind of eternal truth. Vermeer was rediscovered in the nineteenth century and acknowledged to be the great artist he is, becoming an international superstar in a major show that came to the National Gallery in 1996. Religious ideas are regularly forgotten and revived. I personally feel that there is an undercurrent that remains constant through it all, whether it's relevant to the historical moment or not. The individual is the ground where this all plays out, and here there are two aspects to recognition or verification. One is that, as when I have had an experience in my childhood or whenever, the thing I encounter later in life must be true or authentic because it reflects something in me. This is the comfort people take in encountering something they already know, a verification. But then there's the other side, the disjunctive shock, when something is so different or unexpected or oppositional that it is like a slap in the face, a wake-up call. This mode has been dominant in art for the last hundred years or more, but both modes are in constant alternation and circulation throughout historical time.

LH: Then you put up a piece like *The Messenger* in New York's SoHo, as you did earlier this year, and the contrast can be more striking. Your story of being in the Himalayas contains multiple layers in terms of being framed in a tradition: the objects you finally see are historically framed, and physically framed, and ritually framed, and they are there at a particular time of year, so that the whole event has its context. In this country one would have to say, "Well, there's a Bill Viola piece in the SoHo Guggenheim and a block away is a meditation hall and what people should do is meditate for twelve years and then go see this piece." That would be a different experience. When I was there what you see across the street is a Dean and Deluca coffee shop with people getting a nice sticky bun and coffee and coming in and going upstairs to the Hugo Boss awards with some pretty bizarre pieces and then you come into *The Messenger* for fifteen minutes and that's really quite striking and then you go home. I don't know what to say about this.

BV: What if you saw it in Durham Cathedral? Many people who saw it there were just coming to see the cathedral and were not aware it was being shown. I did make it originally for Durham Cathedral, being aware of that context, but in another way I didn't, in that I knew that it wasn't necessary to see the piece there and that in the future it would be shown in different places.

LH: I feel the piece works without any specific context. I respond to the piece, and I find the image haunting without, for example, its title. It could have been called "No Message." So, if I saw it in Durham Cathedral, as a person who lives in the late twentieth century, I might have resisted a little more, thinking I was being told how to read it, as in the "Negotiating Rapture" show. If I saw your piece in Durham, it would be framed in a way that connects with how the figure appears to be an image of Christ. So I'm immediately reading it in that history.

What I'm trying to do here is get a little bit into the seam of what it means to be an artist with spiritual concerns in a secular world. Two thoughts come to mind. One is another thing Eliade once said: "In the modern world the sacred is camouflaged among the profane." It's not that the sacred isn't all around us, but there's a problem about having the vision to see it. The other example, a key one for me, is from Flannery O'Connor, the Catholic fiction writer who used to write about backwoods Pentecostal religion. People would say, "Why, if you are Catholic and this is your spiritual discipline, don't you write more directly about the Catholic Church?" O'Connor said she was more interested in "homemade religions." For her, the Catholic Church had gone through many centuries of winnowing of its practice,

because human beings are fallible and bound to make mistakes. As a believer, you may be grateful for this inherited structure, but if you are a fiction writer interested in the complexities of how human beings do and don't connect with the divine, then the homemade religion, the person who has a spiritual impulse but doesn't have a tradition, allows you to explore all the fault lines. You can see where it becomes difficult and where pride and faith are at odds with each other, and so forth.

My sense of a piece like *The Messenger* at the Guggenheim in SoHo is that it's homemade spirituality. I'm trying here to get at the complexity of doing this work in a situation where there isn't any framing of tradition or ritual or even insight to invest the experience.

BV: I guess the question is whether there is a kind of a ground that this stuff comes through regardless of the trappings, whether it's in a High Cathedral or in High SoHo, or whether we just put it in a warehouse or rent a hall that has nothing to do with fine art, or simply throw it out there on TV or the Internet.

LH: Well, I think spiritual art today has to be able to encompass a lot. There's an old Louis Simpson poem about American poetry with a list of what it has to be able to eat, things like old tin cans and sharks, and spiritual art in America today also has to negotiate a junk pile, the littered street scene. The more you are wedded to a tradition, the harder it is to do that.

BV: I'm thinking of Ryokan, the Japanese Zen recluse. He said, "There are three things I dislike: poems by a poet, writing by a calligrapher, and food by a cook."

LH: That's nice. Now, some place in here there's a question about whether your work has any irony in it. A lot of current artistic practice is willfully deconstructive. It's deconstructive of mythologies for one thing, that is, it is conscious of the way in which the stories we tell are subtly infused with all kinds of hidden problems. I've been working this last semester on Henry Thoreau and I have a double feeling about him, which arises from my own doubleness in this area. It's about being both a believer and a skeptic. Thoreau was mad to become a hero and a mythologizer. His highest regard was for the classics and spiritual texts, and he wanted to write that kind of a book. So you can read Thoreau from the inside and say, "Okay, let's grant his premise that this is a spiritual text," and the work will respond on those terms. But you can also look at him skeptically and say, "This is a guy who is making a fable that works for him at a particular moment in American history." If you look at it historically you can see the places where he has to turn to myth-making because if he didn't he would have to say something more complicated about what's going on in his own culture—he'd have to reckon with the immigrant Irish, for example, instead of scorning them. So Thoreau is ironic about his neighbors, but in terms of his own projects there's no irony. This again is about how the spiritual survives in a skeptical world.

BV: I tend to see the phenomenon you are describing in terms of ecology. Earlier, we were talking about vision and perception, and I was thinking about the fact that these things called eyes exist and that they can perceive the world around us. You can trace their evolutionary development and try to determine how they work and how they codify the world. But you can also take another view and look at eyes as "condensates" of the environmental field over eons of time, in the way that a thorn on a bush presumes the existence of something that is going to eat or harm the bush. The eye presumes the world of light, and in a way is produced by it.

You can stand in front of a painting and look into the painting, be absorbed by it, and then you can step back in a more self-conscious mode and say, "I'm standing in a museum and this is some canvas with paint on it hanging on a wall in front of me," making a jump to another frame of reference. We do this all the time. It's the burden of consciousness. That this phenomenon has come to the forefront of our thinking in the late twentieth century is the result of a process, compounded by the media, whereby a critical mass of information has been reached that makes contexts visible to us that were invisible or inaccessible before. And anything that becomes consciously visible can be "grasped" and manipulated. The whole essence of spiritual disciplines is training the individual to negotiate being both inside and outside of oneself simulta-neously, being both conscious and unconscious or, in the lan-guage of Buddhism, experiencing "non-duality." This is why spiritual traditions have a renewed relevance in today's world.

In today's world, the camera is the emblematic instrument, the icon of self-consciousness. "Look at me, Mom." This is why the photographer Erich Salomon is so extraordinary because he took these photos in the early part of the centu-ry before people really recognized what this new little portable camera was. He had shots of these people infor-mally relaxing at high-society occasions, and they were scan-dalous because all photography at that time was formal. Everyone posed for the camera. So that was a jump in the frame of reference that I can tie in to what we are saying. The trick is that, as you were getting at, if you approach everything in this way then what is real, what is genuine, what is authentic? Can you ever get into Thoreau's world as he wanted you to be in it, or as he was in it, innocently? Have we crossed a line never to return again, or is this a temporary stage and a necessary step to something else?

LH: Untested innocence is sentimental, if not dangerous, but the kind of hyper-self-consciousness now in vogue and the

cynicism it breeds—these are toxic forces. They begin to undermine all faith.

BV: In the course of working, I've felt all along that I never lost faith in the image. My faith was never undermined in terms of an image's ability to engage you in some genuine, real way, on some deep level that's connected to your inner self and that can affect some kind of change or realization. It's easy to be cynical, to say, "I've seen a zillion pictures of the Grand Canyon. Oh, that's just another image." "This is not a pipe." Then, you actually go to the Grand Canyon and you walk out there and step out on that rim, and unless you are an absolute thick-skinned, dulled potato-head, you experience something that you've never seen before in all those photos. They just fall away.

The issue of "being" is the key here. The connection is made through being. If you take the approach of knowledge, which we've done in Western history, you end up with the word "information" to describe this array of events. If you go through being, you arrive in another place, rich in sub-jective experience, which is in a very basic way the primary difference between the Eastern and Western approaches.

Part 2   March 10, 1997

BV: Okay, Lewis, let me take the initiative for a moment at this particular juncture in our conversation to ask you to comment on a couple of different ideas or topics I think are relevant to our discussion so far. I want to talk further about some of the larger issues concerned with being an artist in today's world,

issues that I think about a lot and must live with.

The first comes out of your new book *Trickster Makes This World*. It's about the place of art and the role of the artist in society. Many people feel that there is a crisis or problem with the position of the artist today, that artists have become isolated from the community in which they are presenting their work, like a person behind the glass looking in and commenting on the world they see. And furthermore, artists seem to be talking in a language that only an educated minority can understand or appreciate. This is a sort of pre-quantum physics situation in cultural terms, which comes out of the avant-garde idea of the artist in opposition to the bourgeois establishment, although it is caused by a number of other factors, particularly in America. Compare this to traditional cultures where the artist was a necessary part of the community and his or her work was in accord with and appreciated by everyone.

Yet there are parallels between the two. The artist working alone in the studio is a familiar image to us today; and in traditional contexts as well, the artist usually needs a separation from the group to work—whether it be ritual purification and fasting, the vision quest out into the uninhabited landscape, the shaman's flight out of his body, or the hermit's isolation in his cell. This is often in preparation for the creative act. The key of course is coming back and sharing the wisdom and employing the results of those efforts. This is where differences arise.

Now, in all cases some kind of technology is involved. And sometimes the results are new and startling and in opposition to common understanding. So, I guess my question for you is how do you situate the creative artist in today's world, and is there a relation to tradition, even in the traditionless, adversarial climate of contemporary art? And what is the place of the confirming act and the disruptive act that we talked about earlier?

LH: (Laughing) We could do a book now!

BV: You already have!

LH: Well, one of the ideas in the old mythologies about Tricksters is that they are creative in an unsettling way. One story you find all over the world is that the Trickster stole fire from the gods, or sometimes, as in the Greek tradition, there are two different stories about fire. In one case, Prometheus is the tricky character who steals it from the gods. In the other case, Hermes invents a trick for making fire. He invents the method of rubbing two sticks together in a certain way. Then juxtaposed to this trickery is always the sense that Tricksters are amoral characters. They're not bad, but they are sort of pre-moral or amoral: they live in a space where the ethical situation is unclear or you can't operate by normal rules.

One idea I have about this is that it is an attempt to describe the discovery of new technologies. That is, as the human race moves through history we figure out new ways to manipulate our world; figuratively, every time we come upon a new methodology, a new technological trick—a *techne*, to use the Greek term—it is like a theft of fire from the gods in that it seems to come without our having made any appropriate payment for it. It gives us a kind of leverage which we didn't have before, but then also it's disruptive in that it usually doesn't fit into the ongoing way of being and behaving. So that maybe all new technologies are amoral, and fit into this mythology in this way.

One of the things that strikes me about your work is that television, the cathode ray tube, the whole business of video images, has happened in my own lifetime, and so these are new "tricks." And you are involved in the cultural assimilation of these *techne*, which are potentially disruptive but also potentially beneficial. They are like prosthetic

devices which can deepen our contact with the world in certain ways. You began with a question of individual and community, and in a way I think the community is always resistant to the new trick because it doesn't want to come out of the past, or it is fearful of a potential disruption between the present and the past. But individual art-makers may not be. So, for example, at lunch you were telling me about a new super-high-definition television screen you saw in New York, and I felt your great excitement there. Here's a new trick! Here's something that didn't exist before—and there is an eagerness to make something with it. It might be like extending the palette for you, as if somebody comes into town with a new color.

So, the question becomes: to what use are we going to put our new technologies as they come along? Do you have an obligation toward your community in some way to be the person who translates this technology into a form that turns out to be of communal use? I mean, when your work has a spiritual dimension, is it a reembodiment of the spirit in a new form, or a potential rupture between the past and the present in a new trick?

BV: Well, you've pinpointed something that has been part of me as long as I can remember, the excitement of the new technique. I grew up in the postwar generation. A big influence on me was the World's Fair in New York in 1964–65, which is about as close to industrial Utopia as you can get. For me it was essentially a bunch of dark rooms with images projected in them, a whole series of installations, but cast in a "technology is good, the future is positive" kind of mode. So you had these automated machines in the future ripping up trees in the Amazon and landscaping Antarctica, and nobody was saying how horrific that all is. I was thirteen years old, and didn't see the dark side until later. Now I am quite aware of it, I live with it, and yet I still see and have faith that there is a positive side to technology and images.

One of the things that clouds this issue is that to be truly useful, any technology has to be unconscious. We are in a period where all these new technologies are still very conscious. It's not that we should ever stop questioning, but we need to know that we are using these things to go somewhere, to achieve something, to deepen ourselves and our knowledge. We don't pick up a hammer to have a "hammer and nail experience," we use it to build a house or a table.

LH: People say the learning curve goes from "unconscious incompetence" to "conscious incompetence" to "conscious competence" to "unconscious competence."

BV: That's quite wonderful.

LH: So that, sure, at the end of the learning curve you want to be unconsciously walking or whatever your trick is, but again, as new technologies come along, there has to be some period of conscious gathering up of these things and making them into a new way of being for human beings, "a new way of walking," as the old blues singers say.

BV: Yes, but that's the communal side. We were also talking about when the traditional shaman goes out alone, very often risking his or her life, literally and metaphorically, to leave the group and travel to the underworld and then to return with some deeper knowledge, the purpose of which is to help people. And in a way that is a fundamental process in art, too, because, Mozart, for instance, had to hammer out that stuff on his own. There was no one helping him. As you've said in your book *The Gift*, this is all sometimes quite painful and not fun and very difficult, and yet there's a gift involved that brings something back, that gives something to the group. It's about being given and giving, whether it involves community support and reciprocity, or the many examples of artists who are forever

outsiders, where the only thing that went back into the community was the material result of their work.

LH: You're making me think of one thing that gets said sometimes about the Trickster characters in North American Indian mythologies—that they are parodies of the shamans. Traditionally, the shaman says he is in touch with spiritual powers and courts them to go on nighttime flying trips through the spirit world. In shamanic initiation, the initiate is put through a ritual that involves a spiritual death and a resurrection, and in the resurrection of the "dead" initiate something magical is inserted into his body, like a quartz crystal; and then during later shamanic rituals he can pull this quartz crystal out of his body and heal the sick and so forth. In the Coyote stories, Coyote does things a lot like the shaman, except it's always a total failure. So he tries to fly and he gets the buzzard to take him up in the air and what happens? Of course, there's gravity which rules this world and he falls ignominiously to his death.

BV: Are you sure you're not talking about Road Runner cartoons?

LH: There's a touch of this in Road Runner. There's even a better moment of the parody of the shaman in the Coyote stories: instead of bringing a quartz crystal out of his body when he needs some help from the spirit world, Coyote takes a shit and has a conversation with his turds. And this is one reason my book is called *Trickster Makes This World*, because the stories are about a character who is incredibly inventive but at the same time is inventive in this very worldly way, so that everything he invents has a double side to it. It's both a help and a disaster, which may be a way to describe any human technology. You know, the invention of agriculture is a tremendous leap forward, but it's also destroying the topsoil throughout the world, which in the end may turn out to be a worse disaster. Or in our lifetime think of the invention of nuclear energy. I was

thinking of this when you mentioned the World's Fair: that there has been this optimistic cast to all modern technologies, but the more we look at them, the more we see that they give us a power that is deeply ambivalent.

So again, to talk about artists picking up new technologies, maybe one tradition would have the artist purifying this technology in some way, making use of it and embedding it in our traditions so that it is assimilated, like a kind of food that becomes a part of the body. But another tradition would insist on the ambiguity of all technologies and would see them as simultaneously helpful and problematic. Shamans and artists may need the parody of Trickster to keep them honest.

I saw this ambiguity in your work *The Theater of Memory*. When I came into that room, there were two sounds. One was a melodious wind chime and the other a kind of static, a loud grating noise like an electrical connection that's not being made very well. It's as if in the mythology of high fidelity there is the promise that one could actually reproduce a sound beautifully, but high fidelity also is fighting against the problem of noise, and this piece has in it both kinds of sound. It has the wind chime, which is in some sense a real and unmediated sound, and then there is this static non-sound, so that in some way one is presented with the ambivalence of sound, a kind of beauty-not-beauty. And then I was amused because my *Trickster* book has some stuff about John Cage, and of course part of Cage's interest was to break down this distinction between music and noise. Intellectually, I'm fascinated by this idea, but in fact in the presence of what habitually I take to be noise I begin to react the way I've been trained to react— I want to get rid of the noise. So maybe there's some way in which pieces of yours preserve the complexity of the technology, or preserve the Trickster point of view, which would be suspicious of the shaman making the claim that the new technology will be good. When someone claims to have

domesticated the new technology in a perfected way, the Trickster says, "good luck." That's the Wizard of Oz. You can pull it off for a certain amount of time, but something will happen which will reveal that this is in fact a much more ambiguous universe than we're pretending it is.

BV: Right. So, there's a kind of irreverence there toward things, and that, I guess, identifies the Tricksters with clown figures, or what have been called clown figures, where they are poking fun at the most sacred, revered things. It's like the embodiment of the opposite; everything generates its own opposite. So, high art, then, by necessity at some point in history, would have to generate and define low art.

LH: Yes.

BV: And once that distinction's made, then there has to be a point later where a group of artists come along who are supposed to be fine artists but in fact start making what appears to be low art.

LH: Right.

BV: And that probably has happened at other times in history. It's a bit like what we were talking about before, where the eyes can be both objects that develop in human beings or they can be seen as the result of their surroundings, created by the visual environment. There's a wonderful Rumi poem about a man who comes across a Sufi meditating in this exquisitely beautiful garden with his eyes closed. The man says, "Don't you want to open your eyes and look at this beautiful garden, the signs that God has put before us to contemplate?" And the Sufi says, "The signs I see within. What you see on the outside are just the symbols of the signs."

LH: I think what Trickster would do at that point is to somehow show that...

BV: ...both of them are wrong.

LH: Well, I think that what the Trickster does is to show that a false distinction has been set up. In a way, there's a kind of denigration of the garden in that little narrative. Trickster would try to get you back into the garden with its turds as well as its beautiful flowers.

I asked you this question before about irony. On the one hand, one can treat video as if it were a pure medium through which one sees something else. Or one can treat it in a way that makes you self-conscious of the medium and of the act of seeing. A lot of your work has these multiple levels in it. There's the example of *I Do Not Know What It Is I Am Like*, where you begin with a study of bison out in the landscape and finally one of them notices the camera and stares at us. Then it goes into a section focusing on animal's eyes, getting to a point so close in on an owl's eye that we see the camera and cameraman reflected on the black surface of its pupil.

BV: The blackness of the pupil is the darkness of the space within the eyeball—it is just a hole, an opening. I was always facinated by the paradox that the closer you get to look into another eye, the larger your reflected image becomes on that eye, blocking the very view within you were trying to see. This paradox and the notion of "seeing sight," or looking onto the "soul" of another, was the source of much philosophical speculation in the ancient world, especially by the Greeks, who called the pupil the "puppet," referring to the little person you see reflected on it. Looking into the eye is the original feedback image, frames within receding frames, the original self-reflection.

Actually, Kira first pointed out to me that the sound of sniffling and the bumps and knocks in a lot of my early tapes reveal a presence behind the camera. What would normally be mistakes to avoid, or "bad" techniques, serve to add

the depth of another consciousness, an invisible land-scape behind the camera. At the time, I wasn't consciously concerned that those sounds were there or not. I was more interested in the presence of space carried by the sound, of hearing and seeing what was there. Certainly the work of the avant-garde filmmakers, with their focus on incorporating the properties of the medium into the content of the work, was in this somewhere. Remember that although the camera is a nineteenth-century instrument, it is not an objective eye, and the self-reflective dimension of human consciousness—the "I am thinking of myself while sitting here thinking of myself while sitting here thinking of myself..." phenomenon—is part of the nature not only of the camera but of seeing itself.

LH: Then there are pieces like *Pneuma*, with things at the edge of resolution, or *Tiny Deaths*, where the image is at the threshold of light and darkness, and you can see but you can't see. Or there might be a hiss on the tape, which in other circumstances normally would be suppressed. Again, it's present in the technology and then it becomes present in the art, as opposed to the naive use of technology, which tries to simply use the device as a transparent medium through which pure music or image can be experienced.

BV: Right.

LH: So there are these elements that constantly thwart the viewer's ability to just slide into the image and be enchanted by it in the usual way. In this context, I want to return to the question of the individual and the community and ask for whom do you make your work?

BV: Well, I make my work for someone to see, and this "someone" is one and the same person as myself, but is not myself. (Laughs) I noticed a curious thing as I've been going through all of my old notebooks for this book. The notebooks have different functions. Part of doing them was to keep track of stuff I was interested in and not to forget; part of it was to get things outside of myself, to work ideas out on paper and to preserve the thought processes; part of it was to record commentary and observations, which I would sometimes later use as the basis for published texts. Reading them again, most notably in the commentary parts but throughout all, I noticed that there is a dialogue with this unseen person, this reader. Of course, until just recently I never had any intention or awareness that any of this would ever see the public eye at all. But there it is, this reader, this viewer. I wonder if we could ever live without both subject and object.

I think any artist would say that first and foremost they make their work for themselves. Look at all the disastrous effects that occur when, for example, a group of marketing executives dilute a film director's vision, or when a gallerist talks an artist into making something for the market, or the editorial board hacks up a writer's work. However, we all need an outside reference point in order to avoid the classic pitfalls of individual creative work—narcissism and self-indulgence. But it's a tricky balance to strike. Texts like the fourteenth-century book by Zeami, one of the founders of the Noh theater, called *Kadensho*, written for actors to describe where to put the mind while on stage, and the writings of Japanese Zen master sword instructors like Takuan Soho on how to act by forgetting oneself, have been helpful for me in this regard. Traditionally, many artists were making their work for God, which resolves this problem in a fundamental way.

I am also very aware that I am a public speaker in a way and that I am making my work to be seen. The image I have is of a single mind out there, an audience of one, who is going to receive this stuff. The location of this other mind is the same location as I am at when I'm making the

work. It's all internal. I want people to see my work. I think most artists do. So, there's an interesting kernel in there of ambivalence in this equation of artists and community, in that we are making "private public" stuff.

LH: In *The Gift*, I write some about the mythology of the audience, how different artists have different stories that they tell themselves about who will receive this work. Whitman, for example, invokes a Reader of the Future.

BV: "Crossing Brooklyn Ferry"...

LH: And so he imagines somebody reading him in the distant future, which is an analogue in a way to what you're saying. That is, it is an imagined reader because, of course, it's an unborn person. It's not a reader who has a particular enough identity to constrain him and yet also—though there's debate over this—it's not entirely solipsistic. It's an attempt to imagine somebody outside of yourself to whom you are directing the work. Even if artists don't make art for particular members of an audience, there often is an imaginary audience and the imaginary audience is not exactly you yourself.

I have a friend who teaches Shakespeare who once said to me, "You know, Shakespeare didn't have to write those plays." I said, "What do you mean?" and he said, "Well, the audience for whom he was writing would have taken any kind of entertainment." In any age you can make a Beavis and Butthead movie and people will go see it. It is not as if there's a groundswell of demand for art at the level at which Shakespeare was writing. Yet he had some sense of somebody, the ear of the other, who was going to hear this work. You know, part of what an artist can do is to invoke the best ear possible and speak to it. What that does is to invoke that ear in the listener; in each of us

there are many selves and many beings and many potential respondents, and certain works of art can catalyze in us people we almost knew we were, but didn't quite.

But now let's invert the question and ask, as you work, is there a tradition in your head with which you're having some kind of a dialogue?

BV: Well, it took me the longest time to realize that I was even working in a tradition. I happen to be working at a point in historical time where the "tradition" is to break with tradition—the avant-garde, modernism, an approach in art that has its origins in nineteenth-century France. When I was young I didn't see this as a local historical period at all. I just figured that art is about doing something no one has seen before and artists are supposed to be different and at odds with society. Everything around me in the late sixties confirmed this. Anything to do with classical art, Old Master painting, or making something that my mother would like, was to be avoided as the source of the problem. Video was ideal because it was a radical new tool, the newest of the new, without any tradition—against television, independent of sculpture, painting, photography and even cinema, or so I thought.

What happened over the years is that through my travels and experiences in other cultures, first in Florence and then primarily in non-Western cultures in the Pacific, Southeast Asia, and especially in Japan, and in combination with my readings in ancient philosophy and religion, I began to be aware of a deeper tradition, an undercurrent stretching across history and cultures that's not about the styles and forms, categories and distinctions that make up so much of our approach to the world. You know, the view that comes out of eighteenth- and nineteenth-century scientific thinking, the divide-and-conquer mentality that creates separate com-

partments and imposes a sort of zoology on things. This is still with us today in the institutional structures of art museums and the way we discuss and classify works of art.

The deeper current I'm talking about is the ancient spiritual tradition that's concerned with self-knowledge, that we can see in ancient Greece and in all the great religions, in Early Christianity as well as Siberian shamanism, what Aldous Huxley called the "perennial philosphy," the link between East and West. Your book *The Gift* helped me to see how some of this is present in the contemporary world, a thread that goes back not through institutions but through the hearts of people to deep ancient origins. I also recognized that spiritual history and political history are one. I began to discover the mystics, those who advocate direct knowledge of God through the self, who cultivated individual vision outside of established structures, and were often politically ostracized or persecuted. They became for me not only the key link between my own Western Christian tradition and the Taoists, Zen masters, and Sufis in the East, but also to my position as a contemporary artist as well. Then I began to see the idea of the avant-garde not as a break with tradition, but as a revival of tradition—the tradition of direct experience. This is what so much of the art of the twentieth century has been about, and especially today in the age of no rules, no style, no structures, and autonomous individual access. It was a revelation to see that not only were there rules and guidance for this but there was a whole transcultural, ancient historical tradition as well. The work of A.K. Coomaraswamy and S.H. Nasr has been very helpful for me in this regard.

So the tradition I see myself working from is wrapped up in the individual and the knowledge of his or her place in the world. This is why one of my early tapes is titled *Truth Through Mass Individuation*. The place of the individual in society is one of the key issues right now in America, land of the free and home to individual rights, particularly as they become manifest in the new technologies. I can go on the Internet from the privacy of my own home and, mind to mind, have unlimited access to vast amounts of information all over the world with essentially no guidelines as to how to use that information. All the traditional guideposts are gone. Religion is no longer an effective unifying force to tell us what to do. This is a land of rule breakers with an art based on rule breaking. The moral structure of the community isn't formally intact and certainly not represented in the public discourse in the form of television. Now this all opens new possiblities, but it also creates new problems—basically, the message is that you are on your own to navigate through this chaotic flux of things.

LH: Traditionally, this is where the Trickster comes in; he's the God of the Roads, the guide who knows how to negotiate unknown spaces.

BV: Right. I was wondering, from your perspective as a writer and a poet, and someone who's been very interested and involved with diverse traditions and mythologies and how they intersect with contemporary life, when you wrote *This Error Is the Sign of Love*, for example, whom did you write those poems for?

LH: Well, sometimes you write for particular people, like the typical love poem. It's directed at a specific person. I think when you're young you also write for your teachers. As with children; they need to have their parents nearby when they're playing. It's as if you want to be watched but not watched. Part of growing up is realizing that the watcher isn't quite the person you thought he or she was. With teachers, it's learning that they are particular people and that you're going to betray them, or they're not going to

understand you, or there's going to come some moment when the connection isn't made and yet you know the work is still good. And so then they become part of one's imaginary audience of people at a distance whose work you respect. You think, "I'd like to write a book like the book that so-and-so wrote, or "I'd like to write something that so-and-so would like."

BV: I can remember on several occasions making work with someone looking over my shoulder whom I respect. This brings us to one more thing I wanted to discuss—memory. It's something I know is a very important issue for both of us. I'll start with a quote from the ancient philosopher Plotinus, who said, "Memory is for those who have forgotten."

Then there's this story: Kira and I visited Ladakh in the Himalayas in northern India in 1982. For the first time we were experiencing a traditional Tibetan Buddhist community that was more or less intact, and had been so for many centuries. We visited many monasteries in the region, and noticed the varying states they were in. Some were recently renovated, others were in a state of disrepair. We would go to the morning or evening prayers to hear the monks chant the sutras. Sometimes we were completely transfixed and elevated, at other times, it seemed as if something was missing. I started thinking about traditions degenerating, and then I began to see these monasteries, with their libraries and rituals, as giant recording devices, and the chanting of the sutras day after day, regardless of the level of understanding of the participants, as a huge mechanical reproduction system, ensuring that the knowledge will continue. Where it seemed like a decadence was creeping in, you were just waiting for someone to come along to revitalize them, to stick a pin in your butt and make everyone understand again what it really was all about.

I realized that there is a necessary cycle of decay and renewal in all traditions, particularly those based on one

original person's intense revelation. Something gets lost along the way until one of these characters, like the eighteenth-century Zen master Hakuin, comes along to sound the alarm and reinterpret, renew, and update everything, usually by a slap in the face. It's about remembering in a deep physical way, a carrying back to the source or essence, disregarding the current content as secondary. One of Hakuin's texts was called "Licking Up Master Hsi-Keng's Fox Slobber." Kabir, the Indian poet of the fifteenth century, also does this consistently in a wonderful way. Reformers are always controversial characters, but they provide alternatives by showing the way out, and they regenerate things through rekindling the feelings and energy of the original inspiration and not the rational argument or specific facts.

LH: Is that then an act of memory or is it an act of touching the present?

BV: That's a good point, I'm not sure.

LH: The way I describe it is that it's simultaneous, it's both. That is to say, the way such things are described mythologically is that the truth exists outside of time and that all things decay in time, and the prophet who revitalizes a tradition manages to get himself into this intersection where the present moment is congruous with eternal time. So he simultaneously touches the present and remembers what is true at all times. Therefore, memory in a lot of these spiritual traditions is not memory as we know it, where you're trying to remember what happened in 1954. Memory is a kind of knowledge. It's a kind of knowing and it's knowing things that are true outside of chronological time. The faculty of memory is therefore a faculty that allows you to know in a certain way. This is the famous Platonic set up where you and I were alive before we were born as unincarnated souls who had a certain commerce with the Divine, and in that commerce we knew things that we forgot when

we were born. And the job of the teacher is not to teach us something new, but to help us remember what we have forgotten. And again, that remembering what we've forgotten is not going back in the time that human beings know, but it's a kind of entry into eternal time.

BV: So the connection to the present and therefore the necessary vehicle of the transmission of that knowledge becomes Being itself. In other words, it's in Being where that knowledge is located. That's where it's going to come across. It's not head knowledge, not intellectual knowledge. Is that what you're saying?

LH: Yes. I think that the person who is able to...

BV: ...to embody something rather than just repeat it...

LH: ...and to say it persuasively, is somebody who is operating on all levels—body, speech, and mind. And so it's felt, and it's expressed in a language that is captivating and inspiring. Actually, another way to describe the same thing is that maybe it's not that there are some things that are true at all times, but that in fact this is a time-haunted world, that things slowly change, and therefore the old forms become emptied or no longer fit with what's actually going on at the surface, and the person who is of use to the community is the person who has a kind of vernacular knowledge and is able to make it new in the sense of restating the old wisdom in the vernacular tongue alive at the present, so that people can hear it again and so that it fits present conditions.

BV: Or else you just have the empty repetition of the past.

LH: Exactly. In the last century, a major example of this kind of shift in the surface understanding followed from Darwin's theory of evolution. It so radically and undeniably changed our sense of how we fit into the universe. So then the prob-

lem becomes, how to assimilate this news? Again, you could say in a funny way that Darwin is the Trickster who offers a new *techne*, a new way of seeing what the ground surface facts of the world are, and then the problem is how to gather it up into a living culture where we can make sense of our lives again. So those artists and spiritual people who are somehow able to retell the story now that the ground has shifted, and retell it in a way that makes people feel at home again in this world, those are the useful speakers and art makers.

BV: Now how does that happen? When the message of what needs to be done is disruptive and unpleasant, then how does the creative act become part of living culture? We are really talking in a way about creative acts. These people are creative in the sense that they're not just revivalists, they're really seeing things again with new eyes, and so you are linking that to an eternal present. How does this all happen?

LH: What's an example of the unpleasant?

BV: Well, most things that are starkly new—Jackson Pollock's paintings, James Joyce's *Ulysses*, Duchamp's ready-mades, Manet's *Luncheon on the Grass*, Masaccio's *Trinity*—there are a number of models. I guess these acts will eventually become assimilated over time anyway, whether there is a sensational battle and controversy at the beginning or it just slips in through the back door via tolerance or misunderstanding. It's as we were saying before, there is either opposition or similitude.

LH: Right. There is a little example from Emerson in this country: It's the 1830s and Emerson and a bunch of other people leave the Unitarian Church and try to figure out a different way of speaking about their beliefs; their sense is that it was one of those moments of feeling that the spiritual life of the elders had gone dead. There's an essay on tran-

scendentalism where Emerson says, "I'm sitting in the church, listening to a man give a sermon, and outside the window of the church there's a fabulous snowstorm going on and the snowstorm is exciting and has a kind of authority to it, and my feeling is that the man in the pulpit, his words, have no connection to his life. He has never had a deep feeling or a passionate moment or, if he has, they are not connected to the speech he is giving."

Now for Emerson, the snowstorm is a part of something called Nature, which is sort of an abstraction toward which he gravitates as a place of renewal. But more to the point, what Emerson does is to begin to speak about Nature in a way that insults these older people. He both leaves and is kicked out of the church, and then gives a lecture at the Phi Beta Kappa Society at Harvard that insults the Religion Department. In the meantime, young people who, one has to imagine, had exactly the same experience of sitting in church and being bored to death, pick up a book of Emerson's and read it and say, "Oh, this guy seems to have something interesting to say. And his language, his way of saying it, excites me."

I think the same must happen, you know, with Jackson Pollock or performance art or all these avant-garde moments on your list that are on the one hand unassimilatable. They don't seem to fit and they disgust the elders, but there seem to be enough people around who find these things expressing something they already feel, or embodying their feeling in a way that enlivens.

BV: So there is always the necessity of a community and there always is the necessity, then, of some reflective aspect, some reflexive exchange.

LH: No matter how small a group of people it is.

BV: Or then there is the time capsule model, when someone does something and it is barely even perceived, like Van Gogh having an audience of his brother Theo and a few friends. The time capsule model goes beyond a person's life span.

LH: Well, there's Melville's *Billy Budd*, which wasn't found until fifty years after his death, and then it turns out to be a modernist classic.

BV: Right. Let's talk about a further aspect of memory in culture and tradition, and I'm thinking here particularly of contemporary society. Where then are the patterns of cultural memory stored? Is technology helping or hurting cultural memory? In other words, where do you place recording technologies vis-à-vis the traditional context of memory? We are living in an age of memory, and this is the medium I work in.

LH: I do have some things to say, but to begin, tell me a bit about your own thinking on this. In a way, the conceit is that magnetic tape in all its forms records something over time, and so it is a kind of artificial memory that then allows us to see the past. We can see our own children on tape, even after they've grown up. Do you have a particular intuition about a tension between that kind of memory and cultural memory, or do you see it as augmenting cultural memory?

BV: Well, to situate this, I think you have to go back to photography, which was the first time that light was captured on a surface, beyond the hand of the artisan. You can look at that as being the beginning of the uniquely contemporary phenomenon of making a mark, or capturing a frozen moment that then gets extended in time and becomes a kind of a marker with which to judge the present by.

When I was in the Solomon Islands in the South Pacific vis-

iting these remote villages, bringing my video camera and Polaroid camera with me, one of the things that impressed me was the time when one of the older men walked up to me and said "You look like Mr. Jim." I said, "Who's Mr. Jim?" and he said, "Mr. Jim is a sergeant in the Army who came to our village during the war." I noticed that some of these guys were wearing dogtags from World War II in their shell necklaces. This was now 1977. We were on the island of Guadalcanal. I was a young white American man in my mid-twenties who had just come into their village. I realized that in their minds, when they thought of this person, Mr. Jim, whom I may have looked like, they saw him just as he looked in 1945. For these people, in a world without even a mirror, let alone a camera or a photograph, Mr. Jim is perpetually a twenty-two-year-old guy. At that moment I realized how much photography and my own medium of video, which was young in those days, had radically changed our notion of time. The mirror is present tense while the recorded image is a continuously receding past tense.

That's one thing; then there's video's parent, television. In some ways, I can look at television as the repository of cultural memory, the storage of things that have yet to be decoded. It teaches us that there is no such thing as the fixed past because you can constantly look at *I Love Lucy* reruns. Jim Hoberman quotes Siegfried Kracauer talking about how when grandma leafs through an old photo album, she experiences her honeymoon, while the grandchildren see these people wearing funny clothes and driving strange cars. This is what I mean by "yet to be decoded." And this all becomes even more compounded in a society like America, which itself represents a break with memory and tradition. The new world. Start over. Remake your life. Eradicate or scramble the cultural traditions of much of the rest of the world. Oppress, isolate, or exterminate the cultural traditions of the people who were here before. The

synthetic forms of the movies and jazz, barely a hundred years old, become American "traditions." As the past is being remade, it's also being forgotten; even if it is recycling James Dean or Marilyn Monroe, it is still about the present. Fashion becomes the surface appearance of memory.

Now all of this is certainly exciting on one level, and it has freed up a lot of calcified ideas and fired a lot of the art of the last half century, but my experience with traditional cultures has shown me that a lot is also being lost. Here's an example: think about hearing the theme song from a favorite childhood TV show, or an old advertising jingle. People's eyes light up, it's like an old friend coming back. They still know the song intimately and can sing it out loud. Walt Disney has not only created some of this but now has exploited it as a multigenerational phenomenon. The tragedy of this in the context of cultural memory is that it uses a physiological mechanism built into all human beings to take a stimuli, an image, a song, a dance, whatever, and input it when you are young so that it gets assimilated in a very deep way. This happens in cultures all over the world. Now, if that thing is an expression of the deepest knowledge of the culture, the way that sacred designs on clothing or utensils are to Native Americans for example, or a song is the story of the origin of the group, or a dance is the movement of the creation of the world, then you have something embedded in you that is useful and can give meaning and insight for the rest of your life, even if it started as, and still acts as, an entertainment, such as a funny song to sing. What if that old *Mr. Ed* soundtrack was some model of how to be in the world? What if this cup here that I'm drinking from, with its simple logo, contained a geometric design that had real meaning, or the shape of this table we're sitting at could connect us to the universe in some fundamental way?

LH: Now that's pretty rich. But you wouldn't be an individual in

the way you are, and as an American you're quite attached to your individuality. I mean, we have two cups in front of us and they're each different. And if you think *Mr. Ed* stays with us, I think that American individualism stays with us.

BV: Right.

LH: But I have several things to say about all this. First, there's an old debate in thinking about memory, and it goes back before photography to the beginnings of the technology of writing, and that is whether writing in fact is an aid to memory or not because, of course, before there was writing there was an oral tradition in which people remembered the songs and stories of their community without any other artificial aid. Oral communities have their own technologies for memory—rhyme and meter being some simple ones. And so the complaint that first gets written down in Plato is that the invention of writing kills memory because it means that you don't have to remember in the old way anymore. You remember in this inert way; the things are on paper in a disembodied way.

Here's a simple example in the present moment: We could have a conversation about art in the twentieth century as we are having at this moment and not tape record it. In fact, we are tape recording it. Now, if we didn't tape record it, and later, after dinner, you went to your study and you pulled out your journal and you said, "Now what do I remember about that conversation?" certain things would stick in your mind, and the chances are that they are in some way the important things. They stick in memory for a reason. Actually, there's a wonderful line of Vladimir Nabokov's—"Memory is the mother of the muses because imagination can use nothing that memory has not had the wit to store up beforehand."

So at every moment in your life things are being laid down in memory, and they are being selected as you experience them. There's no way to lay down the entire experience of your day because it's infinite. You immediately make a kind of shaping of your experience. Without that shaping, you'd be swamped. I've actually seen this when sometimes students come with tape recorders to interview me, and my feeling is that they will not get what's important because they will have everything on tape. They will have two hours of tape to transcribe and they can't possibly figure out what matters, whereas if they didn't have the tape and they had to think of three things they heard that mattered, they might be able to do it. Or the other analogy I think of: I learned long ago in revising poetry that I could work on a poem during the day, lay it aside and then, the next day, try to write the poem out from memory. What would happen was that I would in fact have forgotten certain things and remembered other things. And my intuition always was that some useful sorting had gone on during the night, that what I had forgotten could probably be dropped from the poem.

I'm touched by your sense that there are things that enter the memory when you're a child. I have that sense very strongly about certain events which happened to me as a child—songs and stories and places and being in nature—that because they were at the beginning of my life they are authentically primordial, and orient me in a certain way in this world. I found myself standing in my office the other day staring out the window at the trees in Ohio, and suddenly I was thinking about President Clinton's State of the Union address, in which he said every schoolchild should be able to have access to the Internet and do a research paper on the Internet. I thought, what if the president had said every schoolchild should be able to walk into the woods and identify a tree and explain all of its ecological connections? You know, both of them are interesting and valuable things to do, but we live in an age where having

access to the Internet is the officially valued thing. I use the Internet the way I use a library catalogue. It has some clear uses, but I doubt it will ever deepen our sense of what it is to be human. Information is not wisdom or knowledge. Thoreau called most American gadgets "improved means to unimproved ends."

Part of the old mythology of memory is that what the community remembers is the truth. America is an unusual country in this regard for several reasons. Memory is connected to identity. We know from the experience of having a loved one who has serious memory deficit, an older person with Alzheimer's or something, and the question begins to arise, is this the person? There is a way in which we feel we know who we are, individually and communally, by what we can remember. We express this as a virtue when we say "Never forget." But there is a flip side to that: if there is a time when you have to change your identity, if for some reason the situation of your life or the world calls on you to undergo some radical change, then you also need to have forgetfulness. When researchers go into oral cultures with tape recorders and juxtapose the culture's sense of what's going on with a magnetic record of what's going on, they find—no surprise—that in fact the culture *does* change over time. Even if local people say they have sung this exact song since the beginning of time, we know that the songs change over time because the community changes and the world changes.

So forgetfulness is an important part of change. There is a line in Emerson: "Do I contradict myself? Fine. Why should I be a slave to the opinion I had yesterday?" Then he says, "Why drag about this corpse of your memory...?" In a way it's an appeal to the flexible self. To be able to reinvent yourself has a particularly American appeal. For Emerson in the middle of the nineteenth century it was about forgetting Europe. And so what happens in this country is that at Ellis Island people were given pamphlets that literally said, "You should now forget your traditions." An American is somebody who can forget the past.

BV: It's erased.

LH: In Germany, the Turkish workers at a Mercedes plant are never told, "Now you are a German and to become a German you must forget your traditions." They are "guest workers," and they'll be kicked out if the economy changes. And so this is the problem of traditions—they are also intolerant, inflexible, and maintain the old hierarchies. If you are the third son in a family governed by primogeniture and you want to have a farm, then you go to America and forget your tradition.

BV: Do you think that people living in this age of media have a greater fear of forgetting, Americans in particular? Most people, if you speak to them about it, would probably say they're quite concerned about forgetting things, even though it's usually just trivia. We've been given a new model of memory, a new surrogate. Memory, in the form of the computer chip, has become one of the major commodities in our economy. I remember the first portable video machines. It wasn't the live camera that was important, it was the ability to record something and play it back immediately that fascinated us. People started becoming aware of "real time," and all of a sudden the distance between the present and the past was drastically compressed. This was new. It made experience become even more evocative and vivid. And so maybe in this latest stage we are developing technologies that will give us a higher resolution view of memory itself. And this means that it could therefore give us the impossible notion that we should remember everything, when in fact we need to forget to survive in the world and to create.

LH: What happens in America is that there's a great hunger for being in a tradition that makes sense of your existence. There's a longing for a place where you have not only a community, a group of people who have a similar understanding of how they're going about their lives, but also an understanding—a "way"—that has been passed down by people who have really put time and thought into it. There are thousands of pockets where people are still keeping such traditions alive. I do Buddhist meditation with people in San Francisco who do a 5:30pm sitting every day, so right now this group of friends of mine are on their cushions. If you're in a community like that, part of what it does is to give you a different sense of time, a sense of ritual time which repeats something over and over again the way we eat over and over again. Repetition is extremely important for memory. So, when you asked if people are afraid of forgetting trivia, maybe that's a displacement of our longing to be in a tradition where we remember why it is we are alive and how our lives are to be oriented. We should have a parlor game called Significant Pursuit and you'd have a card that says "In ancient cultures there used to be a rule against incest. Is that true or false?" And you'd say, "Oh, yes, I remember that." It would be a game of all the things which have apparently been forgotten in America.

But I want to bring our discussion back to the specifics of artistic practice: are there pieces of yours that have to do with memory, and with the recording and preservation of our thoughts?

BV: They all do in a way. *The Messenger*, for example, works on a level that engages the affirmative mode that we discussed earlier. It reminds you of where you came from. When you see the man emerge out of the water and take a breath, there is a birth every time he comes back into our world. And everybody in the room watching this has come into the world that way; whether they consciously recognize that or not at the moment they're seeing it doesn't matter. It's there anyway. When I witnessed the birth of my first son, I was unprepared for the sheer physicality and the spiritual power contained in that event. I saw mortality created before my eyes. Our new child had just been born and I saw death come into the world. They were one. It was very, very shocking and striking and humbling and profound. And with every breath he took, I was afraid he wouldn't take another. He was such a fragile, tiny, quivering little being, helpless and trembling.

LH: You saw...

BV: I saw the overwhelming fragility, and I saw the sheer power in which the act of birth is manifested. It is quite extraordinary. On viewing *The Messenger*, there is a connection that people feel because they have been there in a certain kind of way and that makes sense to them in their own experience. So both the conscious and the unconscious worlds are available to engage with in the form of artistic practice. Then there is a piece like *Nantes Triptych*, which shows the natural act of birth full on, which is very scary and violent and reaffirming and beautiful at the same time. It transcends any category. And on the opposite screen you have this old woman, my mother, dying. It's not easy to watch, these two heavy things, and yet there is a tremendous presence that's riveting for people in that room.

LH: Let me interject one thing, which is from my own interest in memory, and actually has to do with mortality. It is because of our consciousness of time that we are conscious of our mortality. The organ of memory is the organ that can sense time. I have a sense of the past, present, and future, and that means that I'm sensing time, and to the degree that I really understand what it is, then I'm always aware that life and death are not as distinct as I might have hoped. They're constantly present as a single thing. There are old mythologies of memory concerning

the problem of how the race preserves its knowledge, given the fact that individuals die. And the mythology always is that the individual dies and makes some kind of a passage into the underworld and this passage has to do with forgetting everything you knew in life.

Now, that's a great threat. If you were to believe that the soul is reborn then it would be very useful if you could make this passage without forgetting. If you think of it at the level of the group, if every time the individual dies his or her experience is lost, then the group can never learn from the past, and so the group has the problem of how to preserve the memory of the past given that individual bearers of memory die. And so part of the ancient myth is that the soul passes over a river, sometimes the River Lethe, which strips it of its memories. Then, it's as if individual memories are dissolved in this water and yet flow in an underground river that bubbles up someplace into a spring, and the person who drinks from this spring is then able to become the poet who can speak the past of the group because he has drunk from this spring of memory. So, we started to say that some of your pieces are about memory and time, but what you immediately gravitated to was birth and death.

BV: Right.

LH: Birth and death may not be the first things everyone would think of, but it was what you thought of, and so somehow they're in the same location as memory, and what's being remembered is something having to do with passage and mortality.

BV: Time. The key is that the images exist in these rooms in time. You go into a piece like *The Stopping Mind* and you see a field of flowers and other landscapes and events on four large screens surrounding you. The images are still and silent, presented as frozen frames. Then suddenly they burst into movement, and therefore into life—wild, loud, dynamic, chaotic. I think that someone could see that in a hundred years this field of flowers will still have relevance, and the shifting from stillness to movement will always have relevance for a human being, not only as an action but as a philosophical, moral statement. It's embedded in the human condition.

So there's that other sense of memory in these recordings, a presentation of images that end up placing you somewhere in the context of the physical world and of life in general. And that's something that's in all my work—the act of seeing, experiencing, and its connection to the process of waking up. The wake-up call, the way the medium can echo something in us, engaging our own self-awareness. This is what happens when the process of recording reveals itself. In *The Stopping Mind*, you see a shadow of the cameraman in some of the shots. That's not just about being in the memory, but about waking up from the memory as well. Being aware that you're here. You're a part of it. It's not something that's just a fixed projection from the past. There is this kind of grasping to reach beyond the current cultural situation and the current traditions, no matter how short-lived or long-termed they are so far. I have for a long time now been consciously aware that I've been reaching beyond this present period we're in for inspiration and ideas and even images in some cases. There's an attempt to link with something greater than the last few decades, which is what so much of the culture around us seems to be concerned with. So, I think all those things come together in this recent work, and it has been that way for a long time. I see that it all just keeps expanding out from the center, farther and farther, with no end in sight.

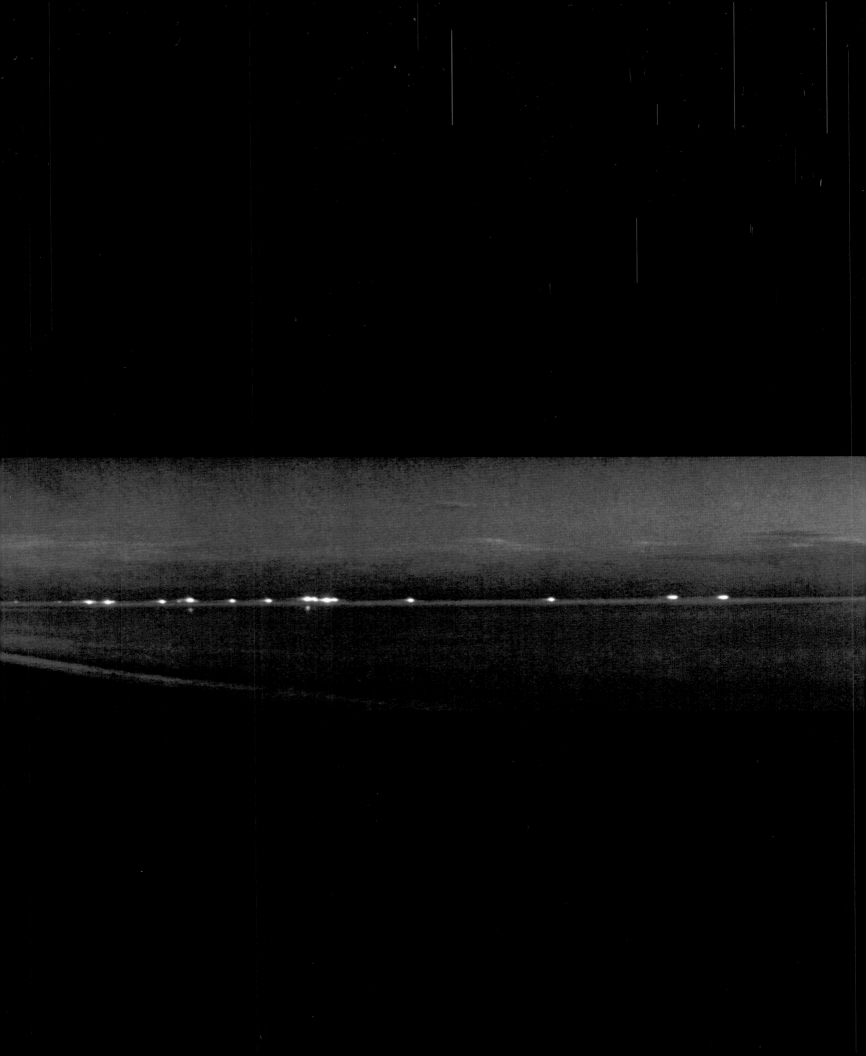

Selected Works 1972–1996: Catalogue

Dimensions are in feet and inches, followed by meters; height precedes width precedes depth. Mono sound refers to sound playing back from a single channel source; it can be sent to one or more loudspeakers. Stereo sound refers to sound playing back from a two-channel source intended to reproduce the spatial separation between individual sound elements in the recording. It is played back on two speakers, respectively, from left and right channel sources. A bullet (•) indicates works in the exhibition; lenders appear in italic type. If no editions are listed, the work is unique.

Numbers correspond to the works described and illustrated in *Selected Works 1972–1996*.

1　• **Tape I,** 1972

Videotape, black-and-white, mono sound; 6:50 minutes
Produced at Synapse Video Center, Syracuse University, Syracuse, New York
Lent by the artist

2　• **Composition "D",** 1973

Videotape, black-and-white, mono sound; 9:42 minutes
Produced at Synapse Video Center, Syracuse University, Syracuse, New York
Lent by the artist

3　• **Level,** 1973

Videotape, black-and-white, mono sound; 8:24 minutes
Produced at Synapse Video Center, Syracuse University, Syracuse, New York
Lent by the artist

4　• **Cycles,** 1973

Videotape, black-and-white, mono sound; 7:04 minutes
Produced at Synapse Video Center, Syracuse University, Syracuse, New York
Lent by the artist

5　• **In Version,** 1973

Videotape, color, mono sound; 4:24 minutes
Produced at Synapse Video Center, Syracuse University, Syracuse, New York
Lent by the artist

6　**Information,** 1973

Videotape, color, mono sound; 29:35 minutes
Produced at Synapse Video Center, Syracuse University, Syracuse, New York

7　**The Mysterious Virtue,** 1974

Installation
Dimensions vary
High-intensity lamp; river-worn stones; woven mat; two loudspeakers; audio amplifier; soundwaves from two sine wave oscillators
Collection of the artist

8　**Bank Image Bank,** 1974

Video installation
Site-specific work
Two banks of six monitors with eight black-and-white cameras in closed-circuit system with feedback; two escalators
Collection of the artist

9　• **Instant Breakfast,** 1974

Videotape, color, mono sound; 5:05 minutes
Produced at Synapse Video Center, Syracuse University, Syracuse, New York
Lent by the artist

10　• **Olfaction,** 1974

Videotape, color, mono sound; 2:34 minutes
Produced at Synapse Video Center, Syracuse University, Syracuse, New York
Lent by the artist

11　• **A Million Other Things (2),** 1975

Videotape, color, mono sound; 4:35 minutes
Produced at ZBS Media, Fort Edward, New York, and Inter-Media Art Center, Bayville, New York
Lent by the artist

12　• **Return,** 1975

Videotape, color, mono sound; 7:43 minutes
Produced at ZBS Media, Fort Edward, New York, and Inter-Media Art Center, Bayville, New York
Lent by the artist

13　**Il Vapore,** 1975

Video/sound installation
12' x 16' x 20' (3.7 x 4.9 x 6.1 m)
Black-and-white videotape playback mixed with live camera on monitor in alcove; one channel of amplified sound; woven mat on platform; large metal pot of eucalyptus leaves boiling in water; live flame heating system
EDITION 1: Goetz Collection, Munich
EDITION 2: The Berardo Collection, Sintra Museum of Modern Art, Sintra, Portugal

14–17　**Four Songs,** 1976

Videotape collection, color, mono sound; 33:33 minutes total
Produced at WNET/Thirteen Television Laboratory, New York, and Synapse Video Center, Syracuse University, Syracuse, New York
Lent by the artist

14　• **Junkyard Levitation,** 1976

Videotape, color, mono sound; 3:11 minutes

15　• **Songs of Innocence,** 1976

Videotape, color, mono sound; 9:34 minutes

16 • **The Space Between the Teeth,** 1976

Videotape, color, mono sound; 9:10 minutes

17 • **Truth Through Mass Individuation,** 1976

Videotape, color, mono sound; 10:59 minutes

18 • **He Weeps for You,** 1976

Video/sound installation
12' x 26' x 36' (3.7 x 7.9 x 11 m)
Waterdrop from copper pipe; live color camera with macro lens;
amplified drum; video projection in dark room
EDITION 1: Staatliche Museen zu Berlin-Preussischer Kultur-
besitz, Nationalgalerie
EDITION 2: Collection of Pamela and Richard Kramlich; courtesy Thea Westreich Art Advisory Services

19 **The Tree of Life,** 1977

Sculpture event
High-powered searchlight illuminates a single large tree from afternoon to night. Five-hour event, Fort Edward, New York

20 **The Morning After the Night of Power,** 1977

Videotape, color, mono sound; 10:44 minutes
Produced at WNET/Thirteen Television Laboratory, New York

21 **Sweet Light,** 1977

Videotape, color, mono sound; 9:21 minutes
Produced at WNET/Thirteen Television Laboratory, New York

22–26 **The Reflecting Pool—Collected Work 1977–80**

Videotape collection, color, stereo sound; 62 minutes total
Produced at WNET/Thirteen Television Laboratory, New York and
WXXI-TV Workshop, Rochester, New York

22 • **The Reflecting Pool,** 1977–79

Videotape, color, mono sound; 7 minutes
Lent by the artist

23 **Moonblood,** 1977–79

FOR KIRA

Videotape, color, stereo sound; 12:48 minutes

24 • **Silent Life,** 1979

Videotape, color, stereo sound; 13:14 minutes
Lent by the artist

25 • **Ancient of Days,** 1979–81

Videotape, color, stereo sound; 12:21 minutes
Lent by the artist

26 • **Vegetable Memory,** 1978–80

Videotape, color, mono sound; 15:13 minutes
Lent by the artist

27 • **Chott el-Djerid (A Portrait in Light and Heat),** 1979

Videotape, color, mono sound; 28 minutes
Produced at WNET/Thirteen Television Laboratory, New York
Lent by the artist

28 **The Talking Drum,** 1979

FOR HERMAN HEINS

Music composition
Performer pounds large bass drum in an empty indoor swimming
pool to excite and interact with room reverberations, with prerecorded natural sounds electronically gated by and concealed within the
live drum beats. Composed for "Dry Pool Soundings," one-week
acoustic research and a concert with three other composers, Media
Study, Buffalo, New York.

29 **Tunings from the Mountain,** 1980

Music composition
Constructed as an eight-channel sound instrument and performed
with prerecorded tape, eight audio transducers with tuned reso-
nant strings and a traditional Japanese *taiko* drum group.
Composed for Fujiko Nakaya's outdoor *Fog Sculpture—A Fog,
Sound, and Light Festival*, Kawaji Onsen, Japan.

30 • **Hatsu-Yume (First Dream),** 1981

FOR DAIEN TANAKA

Videotape, color, stereo sound; 56 minutes
Produced at Sony Corporation, Atsugi Plant, Japan, in association
with WNET/Thirteen Television Laboratory, New York
Lent by the artist

31 • **Reasons for Knocking at an Empty House,** 1982

Video/sound installation
12' x 18' x 25' (3.7 x 5.5 x 7.7 m)
Color video image on 25" monitor; wooden chair with amplified
sound in attached stereo headphones; second amplified stereo
sound source in room on two loudspeakers
*The Art Institute of Chicago; Restricted gift of Barbara Bluhm, Mrs.
Thomas H. Dittmer, Ruth Horwich, Susan and Lewis Manilow,
Marcia and Irving Stenn, Dr. and Mrs. Paul Sternberg, and Lynn
and Allen Turner, through prior acquisitions of the Leigh and Mary
Block Collection*

32 • **Reasons for Knocking at an Empty House,** 1983

Videotape, black-and-white, stereo sound; 19:11 minutes
Produced in association with WNET/Thirteen Television Laboratory,
New York
Lent by the artist

33 • **Room for St. John of the Cross,** 1983

Video/sound installation
14' x 24' x 30' (4.3 x 7.3 x 9.1 m)
In a large dark room, a black cubicle with window, the illuminated interior containing peat moss on the floor, a wooden table, glass with water, metal pitcher with water, color video image on 3.7" monitor, one channel mono sound; black-and-white video projection on wall screen; amplified stereo sound
The Museum of Contemporary Art, Los Angeles; The El Paso Natural Gas Company Fund for California Art

34 **An Instrument of Simple Sensation,** 1983

Video/sound installation
12' x 18' x 25' (3.7 x 5.5 x 7.7 m)
Color video image on 17" monitor reflected in a stainless steel bowl with water; large stone; wooden cabinet and small vase with its optical image projected through a lens onto a suspended screen; vibrating amplified wire; transducer; amplified mono sound, two loudspeakers
The Israel Museum, Jerusalem

35 **Science of the Heart,** 1983

Video/sound installation
14' x 23' x 30' (4.3 x 7 x 9.1 m)
Color video projection; suspended screen; brass bed in a large, dark room; amplified mono sound, two loudspeakers
EDITION 1: Collection of the Frankel Family
EDITION 2: Milwaukee Art Museum; Gift of the Contemporary Art Society

36 • **Anthem,** 1983

Videotape, color, stereo sound; 11:30 minutes
Produced in association with WNET/Thirteen Television Laboratory, New York
Lent by the artist

37 **Reverse Television—Portraits of Viewers,** 1983

Broadcast television project
Videotape playback, color, stereo sound. Forty-four portraits, 30 seconds each, are broadcast in between television programs as unannounced inserts
Produced by WGBH-TV New Television Workshop, Boston

38 **The Theater of Memory,** 1985

Video/sound installation
14' x 23' x 31' (4.3 x 7 x 9.4 m)
Color video projection on large wall screen; 35-foot, uprooted dead tree with fifty electric lanterns in dark room; wind chime; amplified stereo sound
Orange County Museum of Art, Newport Beach, California

39 • **I Do Not Know What It Is I Am Like,** 1986

Videotape, color, stereo sound; 89 minutes
Produced in association with The Contemporary Art Television Fund, Boston, and ZDF, Germany
Lent by the artist

40 • **Passage,** 1987

Video/sound installation
12' x 16' x 54' (3.7 x 4.9 x 16.5 m)
Slow motion color videotape playback, projection on large, wall-size rear screen; built into a small room with a 21-foot entrance corridor; amplified stereo sound
EDITION 1: San Francisco Museum of Modern Art; Accessions Committee Fund: gift of Mr. and Mrs. Donald G. Fisher, Susan and Robert Green, Pamela and Richard Kramlich, and Mr. and Mrs. Brooks Walker, Jr.
EDITION 2: Musée National d'Art Moderne, Centre Georges Pompidou, Paris

41 • **The Sleep of Reason,** 1988

Video/sound installation
14' x 27' x 31' (4.3 x 8.2 x 9.4 m)
Color video images projected on three walls of a carpeted room; wooden chest with black-and-white video image on small monitor, vase with white artificial roses, table lamp with black shade, digital clock; monitor, room lights, and projections controlled by random timer; amplified stereo sound and one channel of audio from monitor
Carnegie Museum of Art, Pittsburgh; Museum Purchase: Gift of Milton Fine and the A.W. Mellon Acquisition Endowment Fund

42 **The City of Man,** 1989

Video/sound installation
14' x 25' x 41'6" (4.3 x 7.6 x 12.6 m)
Three channel color video triptych rear-projected onto a 7' x 7' central panel and two 3 1/2' x 7' side panels with wood frames, in darkened gallery space; amplified stereo sound; amplified mono sound, two loudspeakers
EDITION 1: The Rivendell Collection of Late Twentieth-Century Art, on permanent loan to the Center for Curatorial Studies, Bard College, Annandale-on-Hudson, New York
EDITION 2: Zentrum für Kunst und Medientechnologie, Karlsruhe, Germany

43 • **Angel's Gate,** 1989

Videotape, color, stereo sound; 4:48 minutes
Commissioned for the series "El Arte del Video," produced by IMATCO-ATANOR with Television Española, SA, Madrid
Lent by the artist

44 **Sanctuary,** 1989

Video/sound installation
Site-specific work
Color video projection on small screen within forest of sixteen living pine trees in large industrial space; illuminated by filtered natural light from overhead skylights; amplified stereo sound
Collection of the artist

45 • **The Stopping Mind,** 1991

Video/sound installation
15'6" x 32'10" x 32'10" (4.7 x 10 x 10 m)
Four channels of color video projection, on four screens forming an open square suspended from ceiling of large dark room; computer

programmed random duration and freeze of image; five channels of amplified mono sound, using four loudspeakers, and one small focused speaker mounted in ceiling
Exhibition copy; original in the Museum für Moderne Kunst, Frankfurt

46 • **The Passing,** 1991

In memory of Wynne Lee Viola
Videotape, black-and-white, mono sound; 54 minutes
Produced in association with ZDF, Germany
Lent by the artist

47 • **Heaven and Earth,** 1992

Video installation
9'8" x 16' x 18' (2.9 x 4.9 x 5.5 m)
In a small alcove, a wood column extends from the floor and ceiling, with a gap in the center formed by two exposed monitors facing each other two inches apart, mounted to upper and lower columns respectively, a black-and-white video image on each monitor
EDITION 1: Ydessa Hendeles Art Foundation, Toronto
EDITION 2: Museum of Contemporary Art, San Diego
ARTIST'S PROOF: Collection of the artist

48 **What Is Not and That Which Is,** 1992

Video/sound installation
12' x 18' x 17' (3.7 x 5.5 x 5.2 m)
Seven channels of color video rear-projected onto seven miniature screens in small, darkened room; seven steel armatures extend in a row from wall supporting screens and projectors; seven audio channels monitored through the projectors
EDITION 1: Centro Cultural Arte Contemporaneo, Mexico City
EDITION 2: Fundació la Caixa Centre Cultural, Barcelona

49 • **Threshold,** 1992

Video/sound installation
12'6" x 20' x 40' (3.8 x 6.1 x 12.2 m)
Three channels of black-and-white video projections on interior walls of small, black room; electronic scrolling sign on outside entrance wall bisected by central doorway; amplified stereo sound
EDITION 1: Zentrum für Kunst und Medientechnologie, Karlsruhe, Germany
EDITION 2: Collection of the artist; courtesy Anthony d'Offay Gallery, London

50 **To Pray Without Ceasing,** 1992

Video/sound installation
Site-specific work
Color video image rear-projected on translucent screen, mounted to window facing city street, projected in two successive twelve-hour cycles 24 hours a day; amplified stereo sound
Collection of the artist

51 • **Nantes Triptych,** 1992

Video/sound installation
15' x 32' x 55' (4.6 x 9.7 x 16.8 m)
Three channels of color front and rear video projection, in triptych form; central panel of translucent scrim material mounted in front of an empty enclosed room, adjoining "wing" panels of rear screen material; amplified stereo sound; two channels of amplified mono sound
EDITION 1: *Fonds national d'art contemporain, Commande publique conçue pour le Musée des Beaux-Arts de Nantes, Ministère de la Culture, Paris, France*
EDITION 2: Tate Gallery, London

52 • **The Sleepers,** 1992

Video installation
12' x 20' x 25' (3.7 x 6.1 x 7.6 m)
Seven channels of black-and-white video images on seven small monitors, each submerged on the bottom of a fifty-five gallon white metal barrel filled with water; large dark room
EDITION 1: *Musée d'Art Contemporain, Montreal*

53 **The Arc of Ascent,** 1992

Video/sound installation
23' x 21' x 29' (7 x 6.4 x 8.8 m)
Three channels of black-and-white video, computer synchronized to form a composite single image, projected on a 9' x 22'6" (2.7 x 6.8 m) hanging translucent scrim in a large dark room; amplified stereo sound
EDITION 1: Ydessa Hendeles Art Foundation, Toronto
EDITION 2: Collection of Marcel Brient

54 • **Slowly Turning Narrative,** 1992

Video/sound installation
14' x 20' x 41' (4.3 x 6.1 x 12.5 m)
Central rotating screen, mirrored on one side; two channels of video projections at opposite ends of space, one color, one black-and-white, in large, dark room; amplified mono sound, one speaker; amplified mono sound, five speakers
EDITION 1: Museo Nacional Centro de Arte Reina Sofía, Madrid
EDITION 2: Los Angeles County Museum of Art; Modern and Contemporary Art Council Fund

55 • **Tiny Deaths,** 1993

Video/sound installation
14' x 22' x 27' (4.3 x 6.7 x 8.3 m)
Three channels of black-and-white video projected on the walls of a darkened space; three channels of amplified mono sound
EDITION 1: *Musée d'Art Contemporain de Lyon, France*

56 **Pneuma,** 1994

Video/sound installation
14' x 20' x 20' (4.3 x 6.1 x 6.1 m)
Three channels of black-and-white video, projected into three corners of a darkened, square space; amplified mono sound
Collection of the artist

57 **Stations,** 1994

Video/sound installation
14' x 48' x 58' (4.3 x 14.6 x 17.7 m)
Five channels of color video projections on five cloth screens,

suspended from the ceiling of a large, darkened gallery; five slabs of black granite on floor in front of each screen; five channels of amplified mono sound
EDITION 1: The Bohen Foundation; Promised gift in honor of Richard E. Oldenburg to The Museum of Modern Art, New York
EDITION 2: The Froehlich Collection, Stuttgart

58 • **Déserts,** 1994

Concert film/videotape, color, stereo sound; 28:09 minutes
Music by Edgard Varèse; performed by Ensemble Modern, conductor, Peter Eötvös
Produced by ZDF, Germany
Lent by the artist

59 **Hall of Whispers,** 1995

Video/sound installation
14' x 15' x 25' (4.3 x 4.6 x 7.6 m)
Ten channels of black-and-white video projected five each onto opposite walls of darkened hallway; ten channels of amplified mono sound
Collection of the artist

60 **Interval,** 1995

Video/sound installation
14' x 21'6" x 26' (4.3 x 6.6 x 7.9 m)
Two channels of color video projections on opposite walls of a large, darkened gallery; custom video switching program; two channels of amplified mono sound, four speakers
EDITION 1: National Gallery of Australia, Canberra

61 • **The Veiling,** 1995

Video/sound installation
11'6" x 22' x 31' (3.5 x 6.7 x 9.4 m)
Two channels of color video projections from opposite sides of a large dark gallery through nine large scrims suspended from ceiling; two channels of amplified mono sound, four speakers
EDITION 1: Collection of Marion Stroud Swingle
EDITION 2: Collection of the artist; courtesy Anthony d'Offay Gallery, London

62 • **The Greeting,** 1995

Video/sound installation
14' x 21'6" x 25'6" (4.3 x 6.6 x 7.8 m)
Color video projection on large vertical screen mounted on wall in darkened space; amplified stereo sound
EDITION 1: Collection of Pamela and Richard Kramlich
EDITION 2: Modern Art Museum of Fort Worth, Texas
EDITION 3: Kunstmuseum Basel, Switzerland
EDITION 4: Ludwig Stiftung, Aachen, Germany
EDITION 5: De Pont Foundation for Contemporary Art, Tilburg, The Netherlands
ARTIST'S PROOF 2: Whitney Museum of American Art, New York; Partial and promised gift of an anonymous donor P.4.95

63 **The Messenger,** 1996

Video/sound installation
25' x 30' x 32' (7.6 x 9.1 x 9.8 m)
Color video projection on large vertical screen mounted on wall in darkened space; amplified stereo sound
EDITION 1: The Chaplaincy to the Arts and Recreation in North East England, Durham
EDITION 2: The Bohen Foundation; Promised gift to the Solomon R. Guggenheim Museum, New York
EDITION 3: Albright-Knox Art Gallery, Buffalo, New York

64 • **The Crossing,** 1996

Video/sound installation
16' x 27'6" x 57' (4.9 x 8.4 x 17.4 m)
Two channels of color video projections from opposite sides of large dark gallery onto two large back-to-back screens suspended from ceiling and mounted to floor; four channels of amplified stereo sound, four speakers
EDITION 1: The Bohen Foundation; Promised gift to the Solomon R. Guggenheim Museum, New York

In addition to the institutions listed above, the following commissioning and funding bodies have helped to make the works of Bill Viola possible: Anthony d'Offay Gallery, London; Arizona State University Art Museum, Tempe; Art/Tapes/22, Florence; Cable Arts Foundation Inc., New York; California Arts Council; Capp Street Project: AVT, San Francisco; CAST (Collaborations in Art, Science, Technology, Inc.); Columbus Museum of Art, Ohio; The Denver Art Museum, Colorado; Documenta 9, Kassel, Germany; Electronic Arts Intermix, New York; The Fabric Workshop, Philadelphia; Festival d'Automne à Paris; Fund for US Artists at International Festivals and Exhibitions, a public/private partnership of the National Endowment for the Arts, the United States Information Agency, The Rockefeller Foundation, and The Pew Charitable Trusts; The Solomon R. Guggenheim Foundation, New York; Institute of Contemporary Art, University of Pennsylvania, Philadelphia; Japan Foundation; Japan-United States Friendship Commission; JBL Professional, Northridge, California; Lincoln First Bank, Rochester, New York; The John D. and Catherine T. MacArthur Foundation, Chicago; Massachusetts Council on the Arts and Humanities; The Museum of Modern Art, New York; National Endowment for the Arts, Washington, DC; New York State Council on the Arts; Pacific Ocean Post, Santa Monica; Pioneer Video Manufacturing Inc. and Pioneer Video Corporation, Carson, California; Polaroid Corporation, Cambridge, Massachusetts; Public Corporation for the Arts, Long Beach, California; Savannah College of Art and Design, Georgia; The Andy Warhol Foundation for the Visual Arts, Inc.; Virginia Museum of Fine Arts, Richmond; Whitney Museum of American Art, New York; Donald Young Gallery, Seattle.

Exhibition History

Selected One-Artist Exhibitions

1973   **New Video Works**
Everson Museum of Art, Syracuse, New York.

1974   The Kitchen, New York.

1975   **Rain—Three Interlocking Systems**
Everson Museum of Art, Syracuse, New York (catalogue).

1977   The Kitchen, New York.

1979   **Projects**
The Museum of Modern Art, New York.

1980   **Chott el-Djerid**
Long Beach Museum of Art, California.

1981   **Work from 1976 to 1981**
Vancouver Art Gallery, Canada.

1982   Whitney Museum of American Art, New York.

1983   Musée d'Art Moderne de la Ville de Paris (catalogue).

1985   Moderna Museet, Stockholm.

The Temporary Contemporary, The Museum of Contemporary Art, Los Angeles (catalogue).

1987   **Installations and Videotapes**
The Museum of Modern Art, New York (catalogue).

1988   **Reasons for Knocking at an Empty House: Video Installations and Videotapes**
Riverside Studios, London.

Survey of a Decade
Contemporary Arts Museum, Houston (catalogue).

1989   Fukui Fine Arts Museum, Fukui-City, Japan, a special exhibition within **The 3rd Fukui International Video Biennale** (catalogue).

Installations and Videotapes
Winnipeg Art Gallery, Canada.

1990   **The Sleep of Reason**
Fondation Cartier pour l'Art Contemporain, Jouy-en-Josas, France (catalogue).

1991   **Video Projects**
Museum für Moderne Kunst, Frankfurt.

1992   **Nantes Triptych**
Chapelle de l'Oratoire, Musée des Beaux-Arts de Nantes, France.

Slowly Turning Narrative
Institute of Contemporary Art, University of Pennsylvania, Philadelphia, and the Virginia Museum of Fine Arts, Richmond. Traveled to: (1993) Musée d'Art Contemporain, Montreal; Indianapolis Museum of Art; Museum of Contemporary Art, San Diego; (1994) Center for the Fine Arts, Miami; The Parrish Art Museum, Southampton, New York (catalogue).

Two Installations
Anthony d'Offay Gallery, London.

Unseen Images/Nie gesehene Bilder/Images jamais vues
Kunsthalle Düsseldorf. Traveled to: (1993) Moderna Museet, Stockholm; Museo Nacional Centro de Arte Reina Sofía, Madrid; Musée Cantonal des Beaux-Arts, Lausanne; Whitechapel Art Gallery, London; (1994) Tel Aviv Museum of Art, Israel (catalogue).

Donald Young Gallery, Seattle.

1993   **An Instrument of Simple Sensation 1983**
Anthony d'Offay Gallery, London.

Musée d'Art Contemporain, Montreal (catalogue).

1994   **Déserts**
Collaboration with the Ensemble Modern, conductor Peter Eötvös. Premiere screening, October 23, 1994, Wien Modern, Konzerthaus, Vienna. Traveled to: (1994) Konzerthaus, Karlsruhe; Muffathalle, Munich; Semper-Oper, Dresden; (1995) Palazzetto dello Sporto, Venice; Hallein/Perner-Insel, Salzburg; Philharmonie, Cologne; Alte-Oper, Frankfurt; Konzerthaus, Berlin; Concertgebouw, Amsterdam; (1996) Royal Festival Hall, London; Globe Arena, Stockholm; KB-Hallen, Copenhagen; Auditorio RAI, Turin; Théâtre des Champs-Elysées, Paris; (1997) Schauspielhaus, Frankfurt.

Images and Spaces
Madison Art Center, Wisconsin (catalogue).

In the Mind's Eye: A Sacred Space
Oriel, Cardiff, Wales.

Stations
American Center, Paris (inaugural opening).

Território do Invisível/Site of the Unseen
Centro Cultural Banco do Brazil, Rio de Janeiro (catalogue).

Video Installations and Videotapes
Salzburger Kunstverein, Salzburg, Austria (catalogue).

1995   **Buried Secrets/Segreti sepolti**
United States Pavilion, 46th Venice Biennale. Traveled to: Kestner-Gesellschaft, Hannover, as **Bill Viola: Buried Secrets/ Vergrabene Geheimnisse**; (1996) Arizona State University Art Museum, Tempe (organizer); The Institute of Contemporary Art, Boston (catalogue).

Room for St. John of the Cross
Douglas F. Cooley Memorial Art Gallery, Reed College, Portland, Oregon.

Stations
Stedelijk Van Abbe Museum, Eindhoven, The Netherlands.

1996 **The Messenger**
Durham Cathedral, Visual Arts UK 1996, Durham. Traveled to: (1997) South London Gallery, London; Video Positive 97, Liverpool; The Fruitmarket Gallery, Edinburgh (shown with *The Crossing*); Oriel Mostyn, Llandudno, Gwynedd, Wales (catalogue).

New Work
The Savannah College of Art and Design, Georgia.

Stations
Lannan Foundation, Los Angeles (brochure).

Stations
Württembergischer Kunstverein, Stuttgart (catalogue).

Trilogy: Fire, Water, Breath
Chapelle Saint-Louis de la Salpêtrière, Festival d'Automne à Paris (brochure).

1997 **Fire, Water, Breath**
Guggenheim Museum SoHo, New York (brochure).

The Messenger
Albright-Knox Art Gallery, Buffalo (brochure).

Science of the Heart
Milwaukee Art Museum, Wisconsin.

Selected Group Exhibitions

1972 **St. Jude Invitational Exhibition**
de Saisset Museum, University of Santa Clara, California.

1974 **Kunst bleibt Kunst: Projekt '74**
Kölnischer Kunstverein, Cologne.

1975 **1975 Biennial Exhibition**
Whitney Museum of American Art, New York (catalogue).

9ᵉ Biennale de Paris
Musée d'Art Moderne de la Ville de Paris (catalogue).

1976 **Beyond the Artist's Hand: Explorations of Change**
The Art Galleries, California State University, Long Beach, California (catalogue).

1977 **Documenta 6**
Kassel, Germany (catalogue).

10ᵉ Biennale de Paris
Musée d'Art Moderne de la Ville de Paris (catalogue).

1978 **International Open Encounter on Video, Tokyo '78**
Sogetsu Kaikan, Tokyo

1979 **Everson Video Revue**
Everson Museum of Art, Syracuse, New York. Traveled to: Museum

of Contemporary Art, Chicago; University Art Gallery, University of California, Berkeley; (1981) La Jolla Museum of Contemporary Art, California (catalogue).

1979 **1979 Biennial Exhibition**
Whitney Museum of American Art, New York (catalogue).

1981 **International Video Art Festival**
Theme Pavillion, Portopia '81, Kobe, Japan.

1981 Biennial Exhibition
Whitney Museum of American Art, New York (catalogue).

1982 **'60 '80: Attitudes/Concepts/Images**
Stedelijk Museum, Amsterdam (catalogue).

1983 **1983 Biennial Exhibition**
Whitney Museum of American Art, New York (catalogue).

Video As Attitude
Museum of Fine Arts, Museum of New Mexico, Santa Fe; and University Art Museum, University of New Mexico, Albuquerque (catalogue).

1984 **Het lumineuze beeld/The Luminous Image**
Stedelijk Museum, Amsterdam (catalogue).

13ᵉ Festival International du Nouveau Cinéma & Vidéo
Montreal

1985 **Currents: Transcendencies**
The Institute of Contemporary Art, Boston (brochure).

1985 Biennial Exhibition
Whitney Museum of American Art, New York (catalogue).

1986 **Où va la vidéo?**
La Chartreuse, Villeneuve-les-Avignon, France (catalogue).

Arte e Scienza: Sez. Arte Technologia Informatica
42nd Venice Biennale (catalogue).

1987 **The Arts for Television**
The Museum of Contemporary Art, Los Angeles, and the Stedelijk Museum, Amsterdam. Traveled to: The Institute of Contemporary Art, Boston; Kölnischer Kunstverein, Cologne; Kunsthaus Zurich; Centro Videoarte, Palazzo dei Diamanti, Ferrara, Italy; (1988) Centro de Arte Reina Sofía, Madrid; Museum moderner Kunst, Vienna; San Francisco Museum of Modern Art; Museum voor Hedendaagse Kunst, Ghent; The Museum of Modern Art, New York; Musée National d'Art Moderne, Centre Georges Pompidou, Paris; Tate Gallery, London (catalogue).

Avant-Garde in the Eighties
Los Angeles County Museum of Art (catalogue).

Electrovisions: Japan 87 Television Festival
Video Gallery SCAN, Tokyo (catalogue).

L'époque, la mode, la morale, la passion: Aspects de l'art d'au-jourd'hui, 1977–1987
Musée National d'Art Moderne, Centre Georges Pompidou, Paris (catalogue).

1987 Biennial Exhibition
Whitney Museum of American Art, New York (catalogue).

Taormina Arte 1987. Ritratti: Greenaway, Martinis, Pirri, Viola
Taormina, Italy.

1988   **American Landscape Video: The Electronic Grove**
The Carnegie Museum of Art, Pittsburgh (catalogue).

Carnegie International
The Carnegie Museum of Art, Pittsburgh (catalogue).

Looking with the Whole Body: Six Video Installations
Art Gallery of New South Wales, Sydney (brochure).

1988 Australian Biennale. From the Southern Cross: A View of World Art c. 1940–88
Sydney (catalogue).

...the thousand natural shocks that flesh is heir to...
Ikon Gallery, Birmingham, England (catalogue).

1989   **Einleuchten: Will, Vorstel & Simul in HH**
Deichtorhallen, Hamburg (catalogue).

Encontros: Luso-Americanos de Arte Contemporânea/Portuguese-American Meetings on Contemporary Art: Video Drive-In
Fundação Calouste Gulbenkian and Fundação Luso-Americana para o Desenvolvimento, Lisbon (catalogue).

Image World: Art and Media Culture
Whitney Museum of American Art, New York (catalogue).

Video-Skulptur: Retrospektiv und Aktuell 1963–1989
Kölnischer Kunstverein, Cologne. Traveled to: Kongresshalle Berlin; Kunsthaus Zurich (catalogue).

1990   **Frames: Festival of Film and Video**
Media Resource Centre, Adelaide, Australia.

Life-Size: A Sense of the Real in Recent Art
The Israel Museum, Jerusalem (catalogue).

Passages de l'image
Musée National d'Art Moderne, Centre Georges Pompidou, Paris. Traveled to: (1991) Centre Cultural de la Fundació, Caixa de Pensions, Barcelona; Power Plant, Toronto; Wexner Center for the Arts, Columbus, Ohio; (1992) San Francisco Museum of Modern Art (catalogue).

1991   **Eröffnungsausstellung/Opening Exhibition**
Museum für Moderne Kunst, Frankfurt.

International Art Exhibition Berlin 1991: Metropolis
Martin-Gropius-Bau, Berlin (catalogue).

1992   **Art at the Armory: Occupied Territory**
Museum of Contemporary Art, Chicago (catalogue).

Documenta 9
Kassel, Germany (catalogue).

Manifeste: 30 ans de création en perspective 1960–1990
Musée National d'Art Moderne, Centre Georges Pompidou, Paris (catalogue).

Pour la suite du monde
Musée d'Art Contemporain, Montreal (catalogue).

1993   **American Art in the 20th Century: Painting and Sculpture 1913–1993**
Martin-Gropius-Bau, Berlin, and Royal Academy of Arts, London (catalogue).

At the Edge of Chaos: New Images of the World
Louisiana Museum of Modern Art, Humlebaek, Denmark (catalogue).

Feuer, Erde, Wasser, Luft: Die vier Elemente
Deichtorhallen, Hamburg (catalogue).

Labyrinth of the Spirit
The Hammond Galleries, Lancaster, Ohio (catalogue).

1993 Biennial Exhibition
Whitney Museum of American Art, New York (catalogue).

Widerstand: Denkbilder für die Zukunft
Haus der Kunst and Staatsgalerie Moderner Kunst, Munich (catalogue).

1994   **Beeld/Beeld**
Museum van Hedendaagse Kunst, Ghent, Belgium (catalogue).

Ik + de Ander/I and the Other: Dignity for All, Reflections on Humanity
Beurs van Berlage, Amsterdam (catalogue).

Visions of America: Landscape as Metaphor in the Late Twentieth Century
Denver Art Museum and The Columbus Museum of Art, Ohio (catalogue).

1995   **Death and the Family**
Presentation House Gallery, Vancouver (catalogue).

Five Rooms
Anthony d'Offay Gallery, London.

MultiMediale 4
Zentrum für Kunst und Medientechnologie, Karlsruhe, Germany (catalogue).

Recent Acquisitions: 1994–95
Long Beach Museum of Art, California.

Rites of Passage: Art for the End of the Century
Tate Gallery, London.

3e Biennale d'art contemporain de Lyon
Musée d'Art Contemporain, Lyons, France (catalogue).

Video Spaces: Eight Installations
The Museum of Modern Art, New York (catalogue).

1996   **Along the Frontier: Ann Hamilton, Bruce Nauman, Francesc Torres, Bill Viola**
International Center of Photography, New York (brochure). Traveled to: the State Russian Museum, St. Petersburg; Galerie Rudolfinum, Prague; National Gallery of Contemporary Art, Zacheta, Warsaw; (1997) Soros Center for Contemporary Art/Ukrainian House Gallery, Kiev (catalogue).

Being & Time: The Emergence of Video Projection
Albright-Knox Art Gallery, Buffalo, New York; (1997) Cranbrook Art Museum, Bloomfield Hills, Michigan; Portland Art Gallery, Portland, Oregon; Contemporary Arts Museum, Houston; Site Santa Fe, Santa Fe (catalogue).

By Night
Fondation Cartier pour l'Art Contemporain, Paris (catalogue).

Islands: Contemporary Installations from Australia, Asia, Europe and America
Australian National Gallery, Canberra (catalogue).

Negotiating Rapture: The Power of Art to Transform Lives
Museum of Contemporary Art, Chicago (catalogue).

Portrait of the Artist
Anthony d'Offay Gallery, London.

Under Capricorn, the World Over: Art in the Age of Globalisation
Stedelijk Museum, Amsterdam, and City Gallery, Wellington, New Zealand (catalogue).

Views from Abroad: European Perspectives on American Art 2
Whitney Museum of American Art, New York. Traveled to: Museum für Moderne Kunst, Frankfurt (catalogue).

1997   **Meditations in Time: Selections from the Permanent Collection of Media Arts**
San Francisco Museum of Modern Art.

'97 Kwangju Biennale: "Unmapping the Earth"
Kwangju, Korea (catalogue).

Selected Broadcasts

1977   *Migration* 1976
"Artist's Showcase," WGBH-TV, Boston, September.

1978   *Four Songs* 1976
"Video and Television Review," WNET/Thirteen, New York, June.

Memories of Ancestral Power (The Solomon Islands) 1977–78
"Visa," WNET/Thirteen, New York, May.

1980   *Chott el-Djerid (A Portrait in Light and Heat)* 1979
"Video/Film Review," WNET/Thirteen, New York, August; Belgische Radio en Televisie, October 1983; "Die Matinée," SF DRS, Zurich, December 1989.

1982   *Hatsu-Yume (First Dream)* 1981
"Video/Film Review," WNET/Thirteen, New York, September.

1983   *Reverse Television—Portraits of Viewers*
WGBH, Boston, November; "El Arte del Video," Television Española, Channel 2, Madrid, February 1991.

1984   *Ancient of Days* 1979–81
"Video/Film Review," WNET/Thirteen, New York, November; "The Independents: Dispatches," The Learning Channel, November.

1987   *I Do Not Know What It Is I Am Like*
ZDF, Germany, August; WGBH, Boston, May; La Sept, Paris, January and February 1991.

1991   *The Passing*
ZDF, Germany, October; BBC, London, December 1993.

The Reflecting Pool 1977–79
"New Television," WGBH, Boston, August; "Die Matinée," SF DRS, Zurich, November 1993.

1993   *Angel's Gate* 1989
"Metropolis," Television Española, Channel 2, Madrid, October.

1994   *Déserts*
ZDF, Germany, November; VARA Netherlands 3, October 1995; Arte, France, October 1996; "Alive TV," KCET, Los Angeles, August 1996.

Videography and Audio Recordings

Bill Viola: Selected Works
1986. Laserdisc, VHS; color and sound, 54 minutes. Los Angeles: Voyager Press.

Hatsu-Yume (First Dream)
1989. VHS; color and sound, 56 minutes. Los Angeles: Voyager Press.

I Do Not Know What It Is I Am Like
1986. Laserdisc, VHS; color and sound, 88 minutes. Boston: The Contemporary Art Television Fund; Los Angeles: Voyager Press

The Passing
1992. Laserdisc, VHS; black-and-white and sound, 54 minutes. Los Angeles: The Voyager Company.

Rainforest IV
1981. David Tudor with John Driscoll, Philip Edelstein, Ralph Jones, Martin Kalve, and Bill Viola. 78 rpm record album. Berlin: Edition Block.

Bibliography

Selected Artist's Writings

"Bill Viola: Statements by the Artist"
In Julia Brown, ed., *Summer 1985* (exhibition catalogue).
Los Angeles: The Museum of Contemporary Art, 1985.

"The Body Asleep"
In Gilles Godmer and Réal Lussier, eds., *Pour la suite du monde.
Cahier: Propos et projets* (exhibition catalogue).
Montreal: Musée d'Art Contemporain, 1992, pp. 56–57 in French,
80–81 in English.

"History, 10 Years, and the Dreamtime"
In Kathy Rae Huffman, ed., *Video: A Retrospective, Long Beach
Museum of Art 1974–1984* (exhibition catalogue).
Long Beach, California: Long Beach Museum of Art, 1984,
pp. 18–23.

Reasons for Knocking at an Empty House: Writings 1973–1994.
Edited by Robert Violette in collaboration with the author.
Cambridge, Massachusetts: The MIT Press; London: Thames and
Hudson, in association with Anthony d'Offay Gallery, 1995.

"Sight Unseen: Enlightened Squirrels and Fatal Experiments"
Video 80, no. 4 (Spring–Summer 1982), pp. 31–33.

"The Sound of One Line Scanning"
In Dan Lander and Micah Lexier, eds., *Sound by Artists.* Toronto:
Art Metropole; Banff: Walter Phillips Gallery, 1990, pp. 39–54.

"Visionary Landscape of Perception: The Earth is the Ultimate HDTV"
with Anne-Marie Duguet, Takashi Fujio, and Takeshi Yohro. In SCAN
+ I & S, *Delicate Technology.* Tokyo: Video Television Festival
Organizing Committee, 1990, pp. 141–148.

"Video Black—The Mortality of the Image"
In Doug Hall and Sally Jo Fifer, eds., *Illuminating Video: An
Essential Guide to Video Art.* New York: Aperture Foundation, in
association with the Bay Area Video Coalition, 1990, pp. 476–86.

"Will There Be Condominiums in Data Space?"
Video 80, no. 5 (Fall 1982), pp. 36–41.

Selected Books and Catalogues

Bélisle, Josée
Bill Viola (exhibition catalogue).
Montreal: Musée d'Art Contemporain, 1993. Texts by Bill Viola.

Bill Viola (exhibition catalogue).
Paris: Musée d'Art Moderne de la Ville de Paris, 1983. Texts by
Anne-Marie Duguet, John G. Hanhardt, Kathy Huffman, Suzanne
Page, and Bill Viola, and an interview with the artist by Deirdre
Boyle.

Bill Viola: The Sleep of Reason (exhibition catalogue).
Jouy-en-Josas, France: Fondation Cartier pour l'Art Contemporain,
1990.

Bill Viola: Slowly Turning Narrative (exhibition catalogue).
Philadelphia: Institute of Contemporary Art, University of Penn-
sylvania; Richmond: Virginia Museum of Fine Arts, 1992. Texts by
Melissa E. Feldman and H. Ashley Kistler.

Bill Viola: Stations (exhibition catalogue).
Stuttgart: Württembergischer Kunstverein, 1996. Texts by Martin
Hentschel, Hannelore Paflik-Huber, and Bill Viola.

Bill Viola: Território do Invisível/Site of the Unseen (exhibition catalogue).
Rio de Janeiro: Centro Cultural Banco do Brasil, 1994. Texts by
Ivana Bentes, Marcello Dantas, and Kathy Huffman, and an inter-
view with the artist by Jörg Zutter.

Desmond, Michael
"Interval"
In Kate Davidson and Michael Desmond, *Islands: Contemporary
Installations from Australia, Asia, Europe and America* (exhibition
catalogue).
Canberra: Australian National Gallery, 1996, pp. 71–75.

Duguet, Anne-Marie
"Bill Viola"
In *Passages de l'image* (exhibition catalogue).
Paris: Musée National d'Art Moderne, Centre Georges Pompidou,
1990, pp. 207–09.

. . . .
In *Het lumineuze beeld/The Luminous Image* (exhibition catalogue).
Amsterdam: Stedelijk Museum, 1984, pp. 168–71.

Francis, Richard
"Bill Viola"
In Richard Francis, *Negotiating Rapture: The Power of Art to
Transform Lives* (exhibition catalogue).
Chicago: Museum of Contemporary Art, 1996, pp. 64–73.

Furlong, Lucinda
"Bill Viola"
In Martin Friedman et al., *Visions of America: Landscape as
Metaphor in the Late Twentieth Century* (exhibition catalogue).
Denver: Denver Art Museum; Columbus, Ohio: The Columbus
Museum of Art, 1994, pp. 236–38.

Hanhardt, John G.
  Bill Viola: Fire, Water, Breath (exhibition brochure).
  New York: Guggenheim Museum SoHo, 1997.

. . . .
  "Cartografando il visibile: L'arte di Bill Viola." In *Taormina Arte
  1987. Ritratti: Greenaway, Martinis, Pirri, Viola.* Rome: De Luca
  Editore, 1987, pp. 39–42.

. . . .
  Labyrinth of the Spirit (exhibition catalogue).
  Lancaster, Ohio: The Hammond Galleries, 1993, pp. 12–13.

Landau, Suzanne, ed.
  Life-Size: A Sense of the Real in Recent Art (exhibition catalogue).
  Jerusalem: The Israel Museum, 1990, pp. 176–77.

London, Barbara, ed.
  Bill Viola: Installations and Videotapes (exhibition catalogue).
  New York: The Museum of Modern Art, 1987. Texts by J. Hoberman,
  Donald Kuspit, and Bill Viola.

Mayer, Marc
  Being & Time: The Emergence of Video Projection (exhibition
  catalogue).
  Buffalo, New York: Albright-Knox Art Gallery, 1996, pp. 66–73.

Merrill, Kathleen, and Jenée Misraje.
  Bill Viola: Stations (exhibition brochure).
  Los Angeles: Lannan Foundation, 1996.

*1988 Australian Biennale. From the Southern Cross: A View of World Art
  c. 1940–88* (exhibition catalogue). Sydney: The Biennale of Sydney,
  1988, pp. 266–67.

Pühringer, Alexander, ed.
  Bill Viola (exhibition catalogue).
  Salzburg: Salzburger Kunstverein, 1994. Texts by Freidemann
  Malsch, Celia Montolió, Otto Neumaier, and Bill Viola, and an inter-
  view with the artist by Otto Neumaier and Alexander Pühringer.

Sparrow, Felicity, ed.
  Bill Viola: The Messenger (exhibition catalogue).
  Durham: Chaplaincy to the Arts and Recreation in North East
  England, 1996. Texts by David Jasper and Stuart Morgan.

Syring, Marie Luise, ed.
  *Bill Viola: Unseen Images/Nie gesehene Bilder/Images jamais
  vues* (exhibition catalogue).
  Düsseldorf: Kunsthalle Düsseldorf, 1992. Texts by Rolf Lauter,
  Marie Luise Syring, and an interview with the artist by Jörg Zutter.
  Reprinted in expanded form as *Bill Viola: Más allá de la mirada
  (imágenes no vistas).* Madrid: Museo Nacional Centro de Arte
  Reina Sofía, 1993.

Valentini, Valentina, ed.
  Taormina Arte 1993: Bill Viola: Vedere con la mente e con il cuore.
  Rome: Gangemi Editore, 1993. Text by Valentina Valentini and Bill
  Viola; interviews with the artist by Jörg Zutter and with David A.
  Ross by Gianfranco Mantegna.

Wood, James N., and Teri J. Edelstein.
  Twentieth-Century Painting and Sculpture.
  Chicago: The Art Institute of Chicago, 1996, p. 148.

Yapelli, Tina, with Toby Kamps.
  Bill Viola: Images and Spaces (exhibition catalogue).
  Madison, Wisconsin: Madison Art Center, 1994. Text by Bill Viola.

Zeitlin, Marilyn A.
  Bill Viola: Buried Secrets/Segreti sepolti (exhibition catalogue).
  Tempe: Arizona State University Art Museum, 1995. Reprinted in
  expanded form as *Bill Viola: Buried Secrets/Vergrabene Geheim-
  nisse.* Texts by Carl Haenlein, Susie Kalil, and Bill Viola. Tempe:
  Arizona State University Art Museum; Hannover, Germany:
  Kestner-Gesellschaft, 1995.

Zeitlin, Marilyn A., ed.
  Bill Viola: Survey of a Decade (exhibition catalogue).
  Houston: Contemporary Arts Museum, 1988. Texts by Deirdre
  Boyle, Kathy Rae Huffman, Christopher Knight, et al.

Selected Articles and Reviews

Arici, Laura.
"Vom Umgang mit der Lebensangst: Geburt in Kunst, Werbung, und Presse"
Neue Zürcher Zeitung, December 24–25, 1994, p. 57.

Bellour, Raymond
"An Interview with Bill Viola"
October, no. 34 (Fall 1985), pp. 91–119.

Bloch, Dany
"Les vidéo-paysages de Bill Viola"
Art Press, no. 80 (April 1984), pp. 24–26.

Boyle, Deirdre
"Post-Traumatic Shock: Bill Viola's Recent Work"
Afterimage, 24 (September-October 1996), pp. 9–11.

. . . .
"Who's Who in Video: Bill Viola"
Sightlines, no. 3 (Spring 1983), pp. 22–24.

Daniels, Dieter
"Bill Viola: Installations and Videotapes"
Kunstforum, no. 92 (December 1987-January 1988), pp. 247–50.

Danto, Arthur C.
"TV and Video"
The Nation, September 11, 1995, pp. 248–53.

de Cecco, Emanuela
"Bill Viola: Tra fisica e metafisica"
Flash Art, no. 179 (November 1993), pp. 31–34.

Dorment, Richard
"Life, Death and Videotape"
Daily Telegraph [London], January 12, 1994, p. 18.

Duguet, Anne-Marie
"Les vidéos de Bill Viola: Une poétique de l'espace-temps"
Parachute, no. 45 (December 1986-February 1987), pp. 10–15 in
French, 50–53 in English.

Gauville, Hervé
"La compassion selon Bill Viola"
Paris Vogue, no. 750 (October 1994), pp. 200–03.

Giuliano, Charles
"Heaven & Hell in Real Time"
Art New England, 10 (September 1989), pp. 6–8.

Gugg, Anton
"Kosmisches Rauschen"
Weltkunst, July 15, 1994, pp. 1930–31.

Hagen, Charles
"Back in Fashion, Video Installations"
The New York Times, July 11, 1995, pp. B1–B2.

Hoberman, J.
"This Island Earth"
The Village Voice, September 30, 1986, p. 61.

Hohmeyer, Jürgen
"Flimmern im Brunnen"
Der Spiegel, December 28, 1992, pp. 170–71.

Januszczak, Waldemar
"Closer to Godliness"
The Sunday Times [London], September 15, 1996, pp. 8–9.

Jarque, Fietta
"Bill Viola: 'Hay que acercarse al videoarte como cuando se hojea
un libro de poesía'"
El País, December 22, 1986, p. 27.

Knight, Christopher
"A Something-for-Everyone Group Exhibit at MoCA"
Los Angeles Herald Examiner, June 26, 1985, pp. B1, B5.

Kuspit, Donald
"Bill Viola: The Passing"
Artforum, 32 (September 1993), pp. 145, 204.

. . . .
"Deep TV: Bill Viola's Via Negativa"
Artforum, 33 (May 1995), pp. 86–91.

Lauter, Rolf
"Die vergrabenen Geheimnisse: Bill Violas Video-Klang-Installation
im amerikanischen Pavillon der Biennale"
Frankfurter Rundschau, June 29, 1995, p. 9.

Lebovici, Elisabeth
"L'art de Bill Viola au confessionnal"
Libération, October 12–13, 1996, pp. 28–29.

London, Barbara
"Bill Viola: Entropy and Disorder"
Image Forum, no. 116 (December 1989), pp. 42–52.

Nash, Michael
"Bill Viola"
Journal of Contemporary Art, 3 (Fall-Winter 1990), pp. 63–73.

Neumaier, Otto
"Bill Violas Video-Zeit-Räume"
Noëma, no. 40 (Winter 1995-96), pp. 36–45.

Neumaier, Otto, and Alexander Pühringer
"Buried Secrets: Bill Viola im Gespräch mit Otto Neumaier und
Alexander Pühringer"
Noëma, no. 40 (Winter 1995–96), pp. 20–35.

Nuridsany, Michel
"Les splendides lenteurs de Bill Viola"
Le Figaro, October 15, 1996, p. 23.

Plagens, Peter
    "The Video Vibes of Venice"
    Newsweek, July 17, 1995, p. 59.

Ross, David A.
    "The Success of the Failure of Video Art"
    Videography, 64 (May 1985), pp. 69–70.

Shewey, Don
    "An Artist Finds Poetry in Videotape"
    The New York Times, November 8, 1987, pp. H22, H41.

Smith, Roberta
    "Simple Hardware, Complex Effects"
    The New York Times, June 17, 1994, p. C12.

Sturken, Marita
    "Temporal Interventions: The Videotapes of Bill Viola"
    Afterimage, 10 (Summer 1982), pp. 28–31.

Temin, Christine
    "Captain of the Video-Art Squad"
    The Boston Sunday Globe, July 21, 1996, pp. N1, N4–N6.

Vallese, Gloria
    "Bill Viola: Scelto dagli americani per rappresentarli nel duemila"
    Arte, no. 266 (October 1995), pp. 74–79.

Youngblood, Gene
    "Metaphysical Structuralism: The Videotapes of Bill Viola"
    Millennium Film Journal, nos. 20–21 (Fall-Winter 1988-89), pp.
    80–114. First published for the laserdisc edition of *Bill Viola:*
    Selected Works. Los Angeles: Voyager Press, 1987.

Ziegesar, Peter von
    "Bill Viola at the Parrish Art Museum"
    Art in America, 82 (November 1994), p. 135.

Chronology

1951	Born in New York.
1960	Captain of the "TV Squad," P.S. 20, Queens, New York.
1969	Enrolls in the art school at Syracuse University, Syracuse, New York.
1970	Begins to work with video through the facilities of the Syracuse student union.
1971	Transfers to the department of Experimental Studios; studies under Professor Jack Nelson, who becomes a lasting influence. Founding member of the Synapse video group, installing and operating a cable TV system and color studio in the Syracuse student center.
1972	Creates first videotape, *Wild Horses*. Video preparator at the Everson Museum of Art, Syracuse (1972–74), under David Ross, curator of video art. Works as an exhibition assistant to Nam June Paik, Peter Campus, Frank Gillette, and other artists.
1973	Graduates with a BFA in Experimental Studios from the College of Visual and Performing Arts, Syracuse University. Enrolls in summer workshop in New Music in Chocorua, New Hampshire, and studies with David Tudor, beginning a lifelong relationship with him and performing in his *Rainforest* project with Composers Inside Electronics, a group formed by Tudor in 1974.
1974	Technical director of production at Art/Tapes/22, a video art studio in Florence, Italy (1974–76), meeting and working with established European and American artists such as Giulio Paolini, Jannis Kounellis, Mario Merz, Vito Acconci, Joan Jonas, and Terry Fox. Travels to Death Valley in the Mojave Desert, California.
1975	Meets audio engineer and sound designer Bob Bielecki and works on first collaborative project with him, an underwater soundscape, while artist-in-residence at ZBS Media, Fort Edward, New York.
1976	Artist-in-residence at WNET/Thirteen Television Laboratory, New York (1976–81), working with state-of-the-art broadcast technology, including the Lab's new frame-accurate computer editing system; creates *Four Songs*. Travels to the Solomon Islands in the South Pacific to record traditional music and dance, and to document the Moro movement. First visit to Japan.
1977	Travels to Java and Bali, Indonesia, to record traditional music and performing arts, working with resident ethno-musicologist Alex Dea. Travels to Australia and meets Kira Perov, future wife and collaborator, then director of cultural activities at La Trobe University,

Melbourne. The following year Kira moves to New York and they begin working and traveling together.

1979 Travels to Saskatchewan, Canada, to record the winter prairie landscape and to the Sahara Desert in Tunisia to videotape mirages (*Chott el-Djerid*).

1980 Receives Japan/US Creative Arts Fellowship and lives in Japan for eighteen months to study traditional Japanese culture and advanced video technology. Studies with Zen master and painter Daien Tanaka, who becomes a lifelong teacher.

1981 Artist-in-residence at Sony Corporation's Atsugi Research Laboratories. Further develops work with precisely controlled time structures and computer editing techniques (*Ancient of Days*). Travels throughout northern Honshu with state-of-the-art video camera, recording images for the Sony project, and experiencing rural Japanese culture (*Hatsu-Yume [First Dream]*). Moves to Southern California.

1982 Travels to Ladakh in the Himalayas to observe religious art and ritual in Tibetan Buddhist monasteries.

1983 Artist-in-residence at Memorial Medical Center, Long Beach, gathering images and researching imaging technologies of the human body. Instructor in advanced video at the California Institute for the Arts, Valencia.

1984 Begins long-term project on animal consciousness, spending three weeks with a herd of bison in Wind Cave National Park, South Dakota, and becomes artist-in-residence at San Diego Zoo, California. Travels to the Fiji Islands to observe and videotape Hindu firewalking ceremony.

1987 Travels throughout the southwestern United States for five months to study ancient Native American archaeological sites and rock art, and to make recordings of the desert landscape. Begins working exclusively in black-and-white, using a range of specially modified equipment, recording images at the threshold of visibility with image-intensified and infrared low-light video cameras.

1988 First child, Blake, is born. Starts working with computer-controlled self-generating time structures in installations (*The Sleep of Reason*).

1989 First uses video disc technology as a playback medium for installations. Begins to work with altered aspect ratios and the traditional triptych form in projected image pieces (*The City of Man*).

Receives a five-year fellowship from the John D. and Catherine T. MacArthur Foundation. Records the childbirth process, leading to a long-term project on the universal themes of the human condition.

1991 Mother dies in February. Second son, Andrei, is born.

1992 Produces a series of installations which focus on themes of sleep, death, birth, and mortality. Makes his first work using 35mm high-speed film (*The Arc of Ascent*). Creates a 24-hour continuous window projection (*To Pray Without Ceasing*). Creates an installation for a seventeenth-century chapel, the Chapelle de l'Oratoire, Musée des Beaux-Arts de Nantes, France (*Nantes Triptych*). First private gallery exhibitions, Anthony d'Offay Gallery, London, and Donald Young Gallery, Seattle.

1993 Awarded the first Medienkunstpreis in Germany, presented jointly by Zentrum für Kunst und Medientechnologie, Karlshruhe, and Siemens Kulturprogramm. Receives the Skowhegan Award for video installation, New York.

1994 Invited by the Ensemble Modern, Frankfurt, to create a new work based on the music composition *Déserts* by Edgard Varèse for concert performance; production uses full film crew, a constructed set, an actor, and 35mm high-speed film in combination with video segments.

1995 Receives honorary degree of Doctor of Fine Arts from Syracuse University. Represents the United States at the 46th Venice Biennale, creating "Buried Secrets," five new installation works designed to function as an integrated whole.

1996 Commissioned by The Chaplaincy to the Arts and Recreation in North East England to create an installation for the nine-hundred-year-old Durham Cathedral, the first video installation to be acquired by an institution of the Church of England (*The Messenger*).

1997 Receives honorary Doctor of Fine Arts degree from The School of The Art Institute of Chicago.

"**al-hayrah**" —a constant circular movement around a point mentally incomprehensible. Ibn 'Arabī (1165–1240)

Acknowledgments

David A. Ross

Peter Sellars, Bill Viola, and I made the collaborative curatorial decision to create an exhibition based on the nature of Viola's work as direct experience. Eschewing chronological or stylistic criteria, our decisions in organizing the exhibition were guided by the dynamic spatial and temporal process of encountering the works as individual subjective experiences. We found that we were engaged in a process more similar to composing a piece of music or staging a performance than designing a conventional museum exhibition. Comprised of fifteen installations and twenty-five tapes, the exhibition is a central composition of linked video and sound environments paralleled by a series of videotape screenings. Three of the installations have been selected for individual sites in unique locations out in the community. The Museum installation functions as a complex, new composite work, a "meta-piece." It presents the visitor with various paths through its form, creating a range of possible experiences. And since Viola uses time itself as an expressive element, the installation encourages viewers to find their own pace and pattern.

In this respect, I am particularly grateful to my co-curator Peter Sellars. His experience as a director of opera and theater, combined with a deep understanding of Viola's art, helped create an extraordinarily sensitive and effective installation plan. In addition, his exceptional intelligence and sensitive spirit of collaboration have enlivened and deepened our conception of the exhibition.

This catalogue, like the exhibition itself, grew out of a stimulating creative dialogue that revolved around the experience of Viola's art. The book is composed around two central elements: the direct encounter with the work as represented by a dynamic and striking visual presentation of selected installations, videotapes, and sound pieces made over the past twenty-five years; and a thoughtful contemporary reflection on the work in the form of a conversation between the artist and Lewis Hyde concerning the roots and connections in Viola's work to spiritual traditions and philosophies, ancient and modern, Eastern and Western.

In video art's relatively short history, no individual artist has done as much to create standards for video exhibitions as Bill Viola. For over twenty-five years, he has demanded that museums recognize video's particular qualities and requirements as well as understand that work dependent on sound and image must be afforded the appropriate conditions for viewing and contemplation. At the same time, Viola has managed to build and maintain a degree of professional accomplishment while insisting on an equally high level of design and technical proficiency.

In this endeavor he has been supported by a remarkable team. Of all the people whose role could be considered essential to the project, however, none compares with Kira Perov, Bill's wife and closest collaborator. She has managed all aspects of the production of this exhibition and catalogue for Bill's studio, and continues to be a great source of strength and solver of problems large and small. As a photographer and keeper of Viola's archive, Kira has organized all the visual materials in this book, working closely with the designer, as well as personally shooting most of the photographs reproduced on these pages. Claire Johnston, Viola's long term project manager, has coordinated the monumental task of refurbishing and preparing the works for exhibition, working with studio project manager Bettina Jablonski and Viola's technical collaborator, video and computer engineer Tom Piglin. This same team is responsible for the physical installation of the works in the galleries.

My own efforts have been ably assisted by Emily Russell, whose steady hand and organizational skills are plainly evident in all phases of the project. She is part of the Whitney Museum team, headed by the Museum's resourceful and determined exhibitions manager, Christy Putnam. Lisa Kirt, the assistant director of development/corporate, foundation and government relations and grants, and the entire Whitney Museum development team, lead by associate director for external affairs Susan Courtemanche, worked extremely hard and effectively to find support and corporate underwriting for the exhibition. In this regard we are also grateful to

Alexandra Penny, a great friend to the Whitney Museum. We are indebted to architect consultant Janet Cross for the sensitive and intelligent job she has done coordinating the architectural details of this complex installation.

This book has been organized and produced by the Whitney's remarkable publications department. Once again, Mary E. DelMonico and Nerissa C. Dominquez have managed a complex and demanding project with great skill and sensitivity. Sheila Schwartz, Sarah Newman, Ann Sass, Brian Hodge, and Christina Grillo have done a superb job in the editing and organizing of the publication.

Rebeca Méndez's imaginative design has captured the temporal movement, as well as the visual nature and metaphysical resonances of Viola's work. Her dynamic sensibility and sensitive response to both the artist's and the museum's needs is greatly appreciated.

I am extremely grateful to my assistants, Ja Soon Kim and Kristin Martin, and to visiting scholar Tine Nygaard for her critical comments, suggestions, and focused research work.

Given Viola's connection to Southern California for most of the past two decades, it is highly fitting that the tour of the exhibition begins at the Los Angeles County Museum of Art. I am deeply grateful to Stephanie Barron, coordinator of curatorial affairs during the initial stage of the project, director Graham W.J. Beal, and curator Howard N. Fox, whose unstinting support was particularly vital during the crucial early planning stages of the project. We are likewise indebted to our colleagues at all the institutions on the tour; without their enthusiasm and participation, a presentation of Viola's work of this scope and caliber would have been impossible. In particular, I would like to thank Rudi Fuchs, director, and Dorine M.M.G. Mignot, curator, Stedelijk Museum, Amsterdam; Jean-Christophe Ammann, director, and Rolf Lauter, curator, Museum für Moderne Kunst, Frankfurt; John R. Lane, former director, and Robert R. Riley, curator, San Francisco Museum of Modern Art; and James N. Wood,

director, and Jeremy Strick, curator, The Art Institute of Chicago.

The funding of the exhibition presented a special challenge for the institution. My profound gratitude is first offered to Whitney Trustee Peter Norton for his early and very generous support of the exhibition. With the confidence generated by this support, we were able to move forward. This is trusteeship exercised in its purest form.

On behalf of the Museum's Trustees and the artist, I would like to express our sincere gratitude and thanks to VEBA and its chairman, Ulrich Hartmann. Through generous and enlightened support, VEBA has demonstrated an extraordinary commitment to innovation and excellence, an attitude that pervades the company's identity around the world.

There are other funders who have made this book possible, without whom the project might have foundered. For their generous support, I would like to acknowledge Pamela and Richard Kramlich, Marion Stroud Swingle, Lynn Forester, and the National Committee of the Whitney Museum of American Art. Barbara Wise has provided additional support, and for that and her ongoing support of the Museum's video programs we are indeed grateful.

Finally, I would like to acknowledge Kira Perov and Bill Viola themselves. Together with Peter Sellars, we set out to create an exhibition that would itself function as a work of art as well as a mid-career survey of a remarkable artist. To accomplish this demanded an enormous investment of time, energy, intelligence, and spirit. It is hard to measure or even properly acknowledge the extent to which Bill and Kira devoted themselves to this project, as their commitment level makes words like total or complete seem rather insufficient. Nevertheless, I would like to express, on behalf of the Trustees of the Whitney Museum, our profound gratitude to Bill Viola and Kira Perov and add my own deep appreciation for their trust and care.

Acknowledgments

Bill Viola

This book and exhibition have been projects of passion and commitment for all involved. They represent the hard work of many friends and colleagues, to whom are owed heartfelt thanks and appreciation for all they have accomplished.

There are several people I would like to especially thank for their outstanding work. First among them is my wife and lifelong companion, Kira. Her energy, commitment, inner strength, and intelligence have touched every aspect of this project. She has been there tirelessly at every juncture to ensure that the quality and attention to detail remain at the level demanded by our work. Her discerning eye is behind all the images in this book, as photographer and keeper of our archive, and her thoughtful insights have helped us all stay on track and balance inner needs with the practical necessities of book and exhibition production.

I particularly want to thank David Ross for his long-term interest and involvement with my work and unfailing commitment to the exhibition and tour. He skillfully guided us through the all-too-common obstacle course of physical and financial constraints, while remaining at the same time an active intellectual and inspiring creative force in the project's inception and manifestation. The energy he has imparted to this catalogue goes right back to our earliest days together at the Everson Museum in Syracuse, when video art was being invented.

To Peter Sellars, I quote an old Bulgarian proverb: "If you want to drown, why torture yourself with shallow water?" He took us all about as deep as one can go in a process such as this, and kept us centered on the one and only thing that matters—the place that the work comes from and must return to if we are to be successful in creating a book and exhibition such as this. His generous, creative spirit and passionate intelligence are infused throughout this project. He has played a crucial role in the planning and design of the exhibition, the concept and form of the book, and the architectural floor plan and layout of the works.

One of the joys of my life was to spend two days in conversation with Lewis Hyde. His book *The Gift* changed my life, and his ideas have helped me to understand what it means to be an artist in the largest sense. His contribution here, created when his schedule was impossibly full, has given this book a depth that transcends its function as a contemporary art catalogue.

Rebeca Méndez, our designer, deserves a special mention. When I saw her initial designs for the Selected Works section of this book, I felt that I was seeing my work brought to life on the page for the first time. She was able to capture the movement and flow in the work in a way no one has done before. Through all phases and transformations of the project, Rebeca always maintained a passionate desire and perseverance that the book be special, unique, and creatively approached. Her creative powers proved resistant to compromise and she has clocked up the long hours to prove it, well above and beyond what was expected. For this, her determination and faith in the project, I am truly grateful.

During my absence from the studio for the period of the catalogue production, my long-term associate Claire Johnston and our newest colleague, Bettina Jablonski, both studio production managers, coordinated the efforts to receive, restore, and fabricate the works for the show, as well as the planning and preparation for their installation. Gary Murphy assisted them in this effort. Tom Piglin, video and computer engineer, is overseeing all the technical details, including system design and planning for each venue on the tour.

For over a decade he has designed and fabricated the audio and video systems central to each of my installation pieces. My deepest thanks to them all for their hard work.

In our office there are several special people who deserve thanks. Dianna Pescar, our administrative assistant, worked to research backmatter materials, locating and verifying difficult-to-find items, and has maintained the operation of the office during the period Kira has been involved with the production of the catalogue. Deonne Lindley has had the monumental task of keeping the book work on this complicated project organized and functioning. Sherry Kopach and Corina Gamma have provided much needed support during this hectic time.

Two outstanding people deserve special thanks in getting us through the final and most critical stages of production on the book. Kevin Higa, Peter's assistant, became our full-time coordinator during the critical last month. His quiet, centered persona, organizational abilities and meticulous attention to detail were essential for getting the book finished as we envisioned. Tine Nygaard came all the way from Copenhagen to help in the last weeks, and her experience as a curator, conservator, and researcher, along with her warm personality and gentle manner, completed our exceptional team.

All our concentrated contributions to the catalogue would have been ineffective without the determined efforts of the publications department at the Whitney Museum. Throughout the entire process, Mary DelMonico, head of publications, and production manager Nerissa Dominguez remained deeply committed and personally involved with the creative vision behind the project. Along with Sheila Schwartz, Ann Sass, Sarah Newman, Christina Grillo, and Brian Hodge, they worked beyond the call of professional duty—on both coasts—to stay true to this vision. Emily Russell, our exhibition coordinator working through David Ross' office, has been our lifeline to the East Coast, following through on the planning and organization of the exhibition and tour. Her talents and hard work are greatly appreciated. Janet Cross, the architectural coordinator also working through the Whitney, has brought her technical and creative skills to bear, helping us tune up and improve the exhibition plan, translating the complex layout into finished architectural designs and coordinating all technical details with each venue on the tour.

I also would like to thank the Anthony d'Offay Gallery, especially Anthony and Anne d'Offay and Jim Cohan, who have as always supported my work enthusiastically and have generously helped us to realize the project as planned.

Finally, I want to thank my father for his love and dedication, which has inspired and encouraged me during a difficult time. In the course of this project, he has moved out to Long Beach to live with our family and, at eighty-three and still going strong, has done much to help anchor the details of our daily lives as the schedule became more urgent and hectic. I express my deepest love, admiration, and gratitude for everything he has given and the positive energy he has inspired in everyone working with us.

Whitney Museum of American Art

Officers and Trustees

Leonard A. Lauder
Chairman

Gilbert C. Maurer
President

Nancy Brown Wellin
Vice Chairman

Robert W. Wilson
Vice Chairman

Joanne Leonhardt Cassullo
Vice President

Sondra Gilman Gonzalez-Falla
Vice President

Emily Fisher Landau
Vice President

Thomas H. Lee
Vice President

Adriana Mnuchin
Vice President

Peter Norton
Vice President

Joel S. Ehrenkranz
Treasurer

David A. Ross
Director

Steven Ames

Michele Beyer

Flora Miller Biddle
Honorary Chairman

Murray H. Bring

Melva Bucksbaum

Joan Hardy Clark

Beth Rudin DeWoody

Arthur Fleischer, Jr.

Henry Louis Gates, Jr.

Philip H. Geier, Jr.

Robert J. Hurst

George S. Kaufman

Henry Kaufman

Raymond J. Learsy

Douglas B. Leeds

John A. Levin

Faith Linden

Raymond J. McGuire

Diane Moss

Brian O'Doherty

H. Charles Price

Allen Questrom

Fran W. Rosenfeld

Stephen A. Schwarzman

Norah Stone

Laurie Tisch Sussman

B.H. Friedman
Honorary Trustee

Brendan Gill
Honorary Trustee

Susan Morse Hilles
Honorary Trustee

Michael H. Irving
Honorary Trustee

Roy R. Neuberger
Honorary Trustee

Thomas N. Armstrong III
Director Emeritus

Marilou Aquino
Secretary

National Committee

Mr. and Mrs. Anthony Ames
Atlanta, Georgia

Mr. and Mrs. Charles Balbach
Buffalo, New York

Mr. and Mrs. Sydney F. Biddle
New York, New York

Mrs. Melva Bucksbaum
Des Moines, Iowa

Mr. and Mrs. Paul Cassiday
Honolulu, Hawaii

The Honorable Anne Cox Chambers
Atlanta, Georgia

Mr. and Mrs. Paul Chambers
Trumansburg, New York

Mr. and Mrs. Thomas B. Coleman
New Orleans, Louisiana

Dr. and Mrs. David R. Davis
Medina, Washington

Mr. and Mrs. Peter H. Dominick, Jr.
Denver, Colorado

Mr. Stefan Edlis and Ms. Gael Neeson
Chicago, Illinois

Mr. and Mrs. Drew Gibson
Palo Alto, California

Mr. and Mrs. Brendan Gill
Bronxville, New York

Mr. and Mrs. Bernard A. Greenberg
Beverly Hills, California

Mr. and Mrs. R. Crosby Kemper
Kansas City, Missouri

Mr. and Mrs. Michael L. Klein
Houston, Texas

Mr. and Mrs. C. Richard Kramlich
San Francisco, California

Mr. and Mrs. Leonard A. Lauder
New York, New York

Mr. and Mrs. Kent Logan
Tiburon, California

Mr. and Mrs. Gilbert C. Maurer
New York, New York

Mr. Byron R. Meyer
San Francisco, California

Mr. and Mrs. Robert E. Meyerhoff
Phoenix, Maryland

Mr. and Mrs. Nicholas Millhouse
New York, New York

Mrs. Louis S. Myers
Akron, Ohio

Mr. and Mrs. William Obering
Wilson, Wyoming

Mr. B. Waring Partridge III and
Ms. Julia Jitkoff Partridge
Far Hills, New Jersey

Mr. and Mrs. James R. Patton, Jr.
Washington, D.C.

Mr. and Mrs. H. Charles Price
Dallas, Texas

Mr. and Mrs. Harold C. Price
Laguna Beach, California

Mrs. C. Lawson Reed
Cincinnati, Ohio

Mr. and Mrs. Leopoldo Rodes
San Cugat Del Valles, Spain

Mr. and Mrs. Paul C. Schorr III
Lincoln, Nebraska

Mrs. Donald Scutchfield
Woodside, California

Rev. and Mrs. Alfred R. Shands III
Crestwood, Kentucky

Mr. and Mrs. Robert Sosnick
Bloomfield Hills, Michigan

Dr. and Mrs. Norman Stone
San Francisco, California

Ms. Marion Stroud Swingle
Elverson, Pennsylvania

Mrs. Nellie Taft
Boston, Massachussetts

Mr. and Mrs. Thurston Twigg-Smith
Honolulu, Hawaii

Mrs. Laila Twigg-Smith
Honolulu, Hawaii

Mrs. Paul Wattis
San Francisco, California

Mrs. Cornelius Vanderbilt Whitney
Saratoga Springs, New York

Mr. and Mrs. David M. Winton
Wayzata, Minnesota

Mr. and Mrs. Robert Woods
Los Angeles, California

Notes on the Contributors

Lewis Hyde is the Henry R. Luce Professor of Art and Politics at Kenyon College, Ohio. His books include *The Gift: Imagination and the Erotic Life of Property*, *On the Work of Allen Ginsberg*, and *A Longing for the Light: Selected Poems of Vicente Aleixandre*. His poetry and essays have appeared in numerous journals, including the *American Poetry Review*, the *Paris Review*, and the *Nation*. In 1991 he became a MacArthur Fellow. His forthcoming book about art and culture is entitled *Trickster Makes This World: Mischief, Myth, and Art*.

Kira Perov is an arts administrator, editor, and photographer. From 1973 to 1978, she was director of cultural activities at La Trobe University in Melbourne, Australia, and was curatorial assistant for video art at the Long Beach Museum of Art in California from 1983 to 84. She has worked closely with Bill Viola, her partner and husband since 1978, managing the production of his videotapes, installations, publications, and photo archive, as well as coordinating his exhibitions worldwide. Her photographic documentation of artists' work, including Viola's, as well as her personal photographs, have been exhibited and published internationally in books, magazines, and museum catalogues.

David A. Ross is director of the Whitney Museum of American Art.

Peter Sellars, theater, opera, and television director, has directed more than one hundred productions across America and abroad. Before becoming director of the American National Theater at the Kennedy Center in Washington, D.C., he studied in Japan, China, and India. A frequent guest at the Salzburg and Glyndebourne Festivals, he has specialized in contemporary operas, including Olivier Messiaen's *St. François d'Assise*, Igor Stravinsky's *The Rake's Progress*, György Ligeti's *Le Grand Macabre*, and with choreographer Mark Morris, the premiere of John Adams and Alice Goodman's *Nixon in China* and *The Death of Klinghoffer*. He was artistic director of the 1990 and 1993 Los Angeles Festivals and he is a professor in the world arts and cultures department at the University of California at Los Angeles.

Library of Congress Cataloging-in-Publication Data

Ross, David A.
  David A. Ross and Peter Sellars ; with contributions by Lewis Hyde ... [et al.].
  p. cm.
  "In association with Flammarion, Paris-New York."
  Includes bibliographical references.
  ISBN 0–87427–114–2
  1. Viola, Bill, 1951—Contributions in video art.
      I. Ross, David A. II. Hyde, Lewis. III. Whitney Museum of
      American Art
N6537.V56A35   1997
700'.92—dc21

                                                              97–26976
                                                              CIP

ISBN 0-87427–114–2   paper (Whitney)
ISBN 2-08013–645–3   cloth (Flammarion)

                      Flammarion
                      26 rue Racine, 75006 Paris

                      200 Park Avenue South, Suite 1406
                      New York, New York 10003

                      Numéro d'édition: FA364502
                      Dépôt légal: October 1997

Published by: Whitney Museum of American Art
                      945 Madison Avenue
                      New York, New York 10021

Front and back cover: *The Crossing*, 1996
Pages 3–9, 208–14: *The Passing*, 1991
Pages 16–17: Bill Viola at Zabriskie Point, Death Valley
Pages 31–38: *The Messenger*, 1996
Pages 128–41: *The Crossing*, 1996
Pages 166–70, 175–80: Camera pan from *Hatsu-Yume (First Dream)*, 1981. Festival at
Osorezan-Bodaiji temple in the caldera of sacred Osorezan Mountain, the gathering place
of the spirits of the dead in northern Japan.
Pages 171–74: Camera pan from *The Passing*, 1991, Bonneville Salt Flats, Utah

All texts and images by Bill Viola ©1997 Bill Viola
©1997 Whitney Museum of American Art
All rights reserved. No part of this publication may be reproduced in any form or by any
means, electronic, photocopy, information retrieval system, or otherwise without written
permission from the Whitney Museum of American Art.

This publication was organized at the Whitney Museum by Mary E. DelMonico, *Head, Publications*; Sheila Schwartz, *Editor*; Nerissa C. Dominguez, *Production Manager*; Ann Sass, *Copy Editor*; Sarah Newman, *Senior Assistant*; Brian Hodge, *Assistant/Design*; Christina Grillo, *Assistant*; Soonyoung Kwon, Jennifer Bilenker, and Margaret Cameron, *Interns*.

Editor:	Kira Perov
Design:	Rebeca Méndez, *balam@earthlink.net*
Design assistance:	Bele Ducke, Yoon Lee, and Susana Mendive
Production assistance:	Adam Eeuwens, Kevin Higa, Tine Nygaard, and Dianna Pescar
Consultant:	Emily Russell
Separations:	DeskTop Produktion Bucher GmbH, Stuttgart, F. Bucher/R. Strecker
Printing:	Dr. Cantz'sche Druckerei, Ostfildern
Binding:	Bramsche Buchbinder Betriebe GmbH

Image sequences, pp. 31–38, 128–41; camera pans, pp. 166–80 were created by Bill Viola for this book.

Photograph and Reproduction Credits: All photographs by Kira Perov except: Alinari/Art Resource, NY: 26; Per-Anders Allsten/Courtesy Moderna Museet, Stockholm: 100; Shigeo Anzai: 58 (bottom); Bob Bielecki and Greg Shefrin: 61 (top); Philip S. Block: 46, 47 (bottom); Eduardo Calderón: 101 (top and bottom); Charles Duprat: 112, 113; Robert Keziere/Courtesy Ydessa Hendeles Foundation: 98 (top), 99 (top left, top right); Courtesy The Kobal Collection: 25; Robert Lorenz: 23; Gary McKinnis: 106, 107; Gianni Melotti: 53; Roman Mensing: 116, 117, 120, 121; ©1997 Bruce Nauman/Artists Rights Society (ARS), New York: 22; Kira Perov/Squidds & Nunns: 77, 82; Richard Stoner/Courtesy The Carnegie Museum of Art: 88–89 (top); Nic Tenwiggenhorn: 104; Frank J. Thomas, courtesy Bruce Nauman: 22; Bill Viola: 47 (top); Edward Woodman: 125

Adobe Photoshop™ work: Julie Grosse: 105; Joseph Richard Negro: 166–80

Black-and-white photoprinter: Danny Kay Johnson

Drawing on p. 71 (bottom left): Bill Viola

Printed and bound in Germany

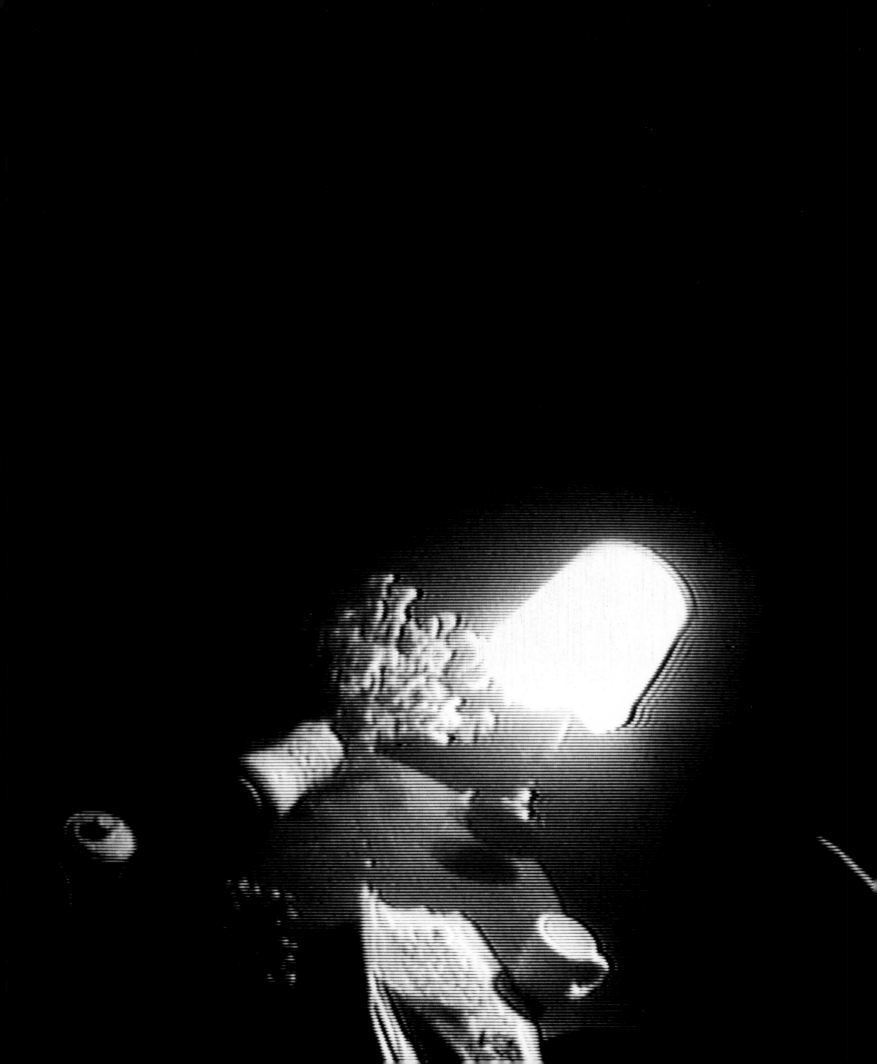

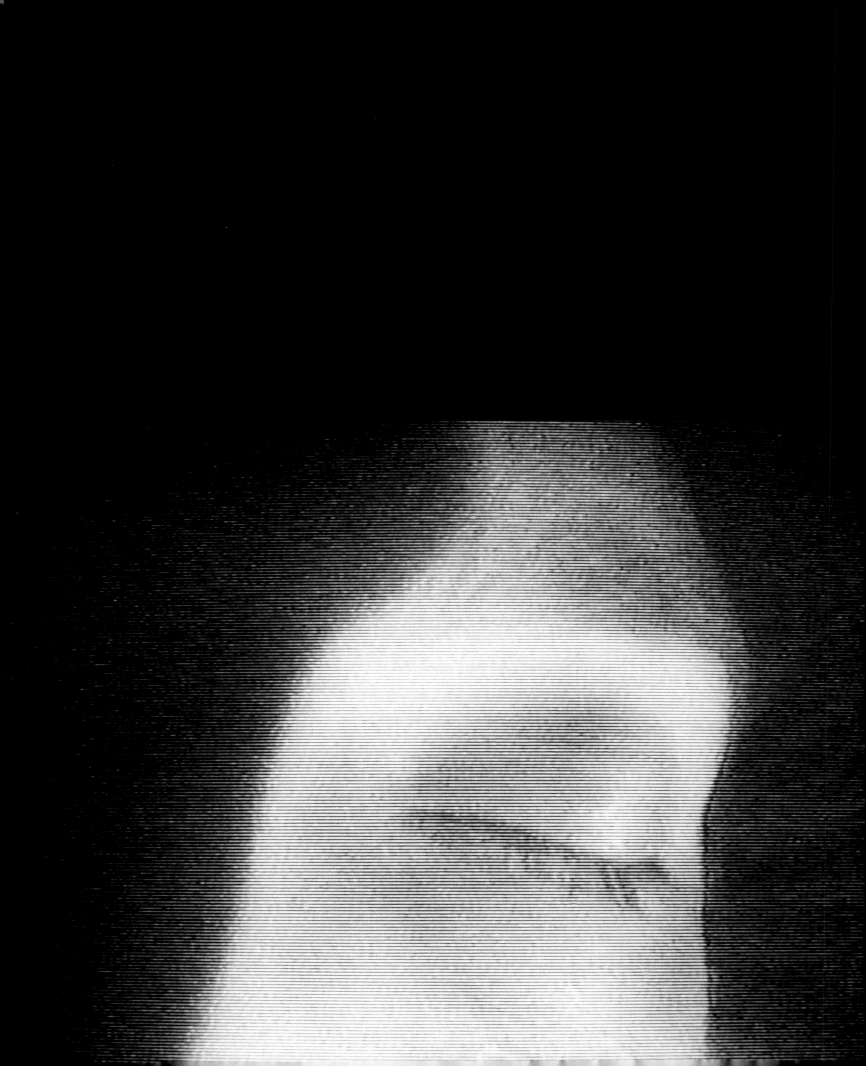

W9-AOX-147